ADVANCE PRAISE FOR *WHEN WE COULD NOT SEE THE MOON*

"*When We Could Not See the Moon* is a testament to the strength of faith and family in the face of adversity. As Jon and Tracy recount the ordeal of their daughter Hanna's imprisonment in Egypt, their trust in God's love and providence shines through. Guided by the truth that 'in all things God works for the good of those who love Him' (Romans 8:28), the Willems family harnessed their faith to find the courage and resilience needed to bring Hanna home. From the timing of Hanna's judge issuing her release on bail to the compassion of her cellmate Inara whose kindness reflected God's light in the darkest of places, this true story reminds us that God is always by our side. Jon and Tracy's vulnerable reflections drive home the power of faith—not as a magic shield against hardship but as a foundation from which we can weather any storm, knowing we are held in the arms of a loving God. *When We Could Not See the Moon* will reaffirm your belief in miracles and inspire you to trust more deeply in God's plan."

—Shaan Sharma, actor playing "Shmuel" on *The Chosen*

"*When We Could Not See the Moon* starts as any normal day and builds to a maximum crescendo. It truly demonstrates the necessity of justice, the exigency of human dignity, the purpose of family, and the power of prayer."

—Lawrence Wasden, former Idaho attorney general

"This is a must-read for any parent or anyone who has ever wanted to travel beyond the borders of the United States. *When We Could Not See the Moon* is a riveting story that combines friendship and faith with so many twists and turns that any reader will rethink their perspective when situations are beyond their control."

—Maryanna Young, CEO of Aloha Publishing

READERS' PRAISE FOR *WHEN WE COULD NOT SEE THE MOON*

"I couldn't put it down. It is every parent's nightmare—to have something like this happen to their child—but the strength and support that this family found in their faith and in the community of friends and contacts was amazing."

—Marsha Abel

"The pain and gut-wrenching emotions are so palpable. Faith will not shield us from hardship but will get us through. This book is a testament to the human spirit."

—Chris Dixon

"Life takes us places we never expect . . . This compelling story of fear, tears, friendship, and faith was personal—it was my family. Experience the nightmare of my daughter and her husband, of my granddaughter who was incarcerated in Egypt, and of the many people who answered the call to help. I had the opportunity to see the hand of God in it all."

—Sidney Bartlett, mom and grandma of the family

"This is a deeply moving account of when our friends were tested by the harshest of realities. During that time, I found myself daily at temple lifting their daughter up in prayer. It is a testament to faith being affirmed during very challenging times."

—N. Goyal

WHEN WE COULD NOT SEE THE MOON

WHEN WE COULD NOT SEE THE MOON

OUR DAUGHTER LOCKED AWAY
IN A FOREIGN JAIL

A TRUE STORY OF FAITH AS TOLD BY
THE FAMILY TO SAVANNAH SPIDALIERI

Ballast Books, LLC
www.ballastbooks.com

When We Could Not See the Moon
Our Daughter Locked Away in a Foreign Jail

A true story of faith as told by the family to Savannah Spidalieri

Written by Savannah Spidalieri

Willson, Meredith. 1953. "I See the Moon." The Mariners. Columbia Records.

ISBN: 978-1-962202-74-9

Printed in Hong Kong

Published by Ballast Books

www.ballastbooks.com

For more information, bulk orders, appearances, or speaking requests,
please email info@ballastbooks.com
or visit www.whenwecouldnotseethemoon.com

DEDICATION

To the women who touched our daughter's heart and all those who worked diligently on her behalf.

PART ONE

THE DROWNING MAN

A devout man found himself in the middle of the ocean, no land in sight. Without a miracle, he would surely drown. So, being a man of faith, he prayed fervently to God to please spare his life and send a miracle. And—being a man of faith—after placing the situation in God's hands, he felt reassured he would, in fact, be saved.

After some time, a fishing boat came along, and a fisherman threw out a rope.

"Grab it!" the fisherman yelled to the drowning man.

But the drowning man only waved him off. "I've asked God for help, and He will save me," he said to the fisherman.

The fisherman stared in disbelief, watching the drowning man as he drifted away.

Some time later, another boat happened upon the drowning man. A group of whale watchers aboard the boat saw the man clearly struggling to stay afloat and threw out a life preserver.

"Grab it!" the group yelled to the drowning man. "We'll pull you aboard!"

When the man didn't reach out, they said, "At least take the life preserver; it will keep you afloat!"

But the drowning man only shook his head. "I've asked God for help, and He will save me," he answered, and he tossed the life preserver back into the boat.

Later, as the man began to tire of treading water, a rescue helicopter appeared overhead, and a ladder dropped out of the sky.

"Climb up!" a voice bellowed from above. "We've come to rescue you."

But though the man's arms and legs were tired, his faith was steadfast. "God will save me!" he shouted to the helicopter.

Alone in the water once again, the drowning man waited for his miracle. He waited as day turned to night and the moon rose high in the sky above him.

He waited.

And he waited.

And he drowned.

Now, face to face with God, the man was in impassioned disbelief.

"I asked you for help!" the man of unwavering faith shouted at his would-be savior. "Where were you?" he demanded.

God looked at the man, astounded. "I sent you a fisherman, a life preserver . . . a helicopter! And every time, you turned them away. What, exactly, were you waiting for?"

MONDAY, FEBRUARY 22ND

12:30 A.M.
TRACY

The text came after midnight. As every parent knows, the midnight call or text is never the one you want to receive. But it was one I felt in my bones was coming.

It started as a little nagging worry, as we hadn't heard from Hanna when her plane had touched down. Then, it grew steadily as the hours, then days, passed by and she did not check in. Not to say she was settled into her lodging or to send a photo as she toasted with friends to celebrate the start of her yearlong adventure abroad or even to admit she was already missing home. Finally, that nagging worry had grown into the foreboding anxiety that had ensured when that midnight text did arrive, I was awake and waiting for it.

The buzz of my phone across the room. The leap in my chest, cutting off my breath. The silent plea as I reached for the phone on the table—*please be from Hanna*. I wanted more than anything to feel that unique mixture of both relief and frustration. I wanted to finally know she was safe, and I wanted to be angry with her for not checking in sooner.

But it wasn't Hanna's name on the screen. It was Taylor, our youngest daughter.

Can you please call me in the morning? I have some news about Hanna.

I didn't wait until morning. I barely waited to read the whole text. It was after midnight, and sleep was not coming for me. I wouldn't sleep at all that night. In fact, I wouldn't sleep well for many more.

TWO NIGHTS EARLIER FRIDAY, FEBRUARY 19TH

SHORTLY BEFORE MIDNIGHT
JON

Next chapter begins today!

Hanna's message had come through just as we were preparing to turn in for the night. We'd arrived at the cabin hours earlier—in the dark, as was usual that time of year. And—as was usual that time of year—we'd spent several hours settling in. Our weekend retreat nestled in the deep woods of Idaho is not without its own set of chores and maintenance responsibilities—especially during the winter months.

Idaho snow is as dense and unrelenting as it is beautiful. Often, when we share photos of our wintery accumulation with friends and family in various parts of the world—photos of our cabin picturesquely buried under drifts several feet deep—they marvel at the sheer amount of it.

Snow in this part of Idaho is more than a part of life. In many ways it *is* life. Two of our major industries—tourism and agriculture—rely on a good snowfall each year. Millions of skiers, snowboarders, and other winter thrill-seekers descend upon Idaho's numerous resort spots each year to carve fresh tracks in the abundance of seasonal snow. Those in agriculture are counting on a dense snowpack and good runoff to replenish reservoirs that will feed the state's agricultural areas through another long, dry summer.

I, for one, find myself firmly in both camps. I love to get out to the cabin after a good snowfall to do some snowmobiling, and I also know how important that end-of-season runoff is for the potato industry—the very industry that brought me to Idaho in the first place. So, when the snow comes, we're grateful for its beautiful inconvenience. We work through it—literally.

Tracy and I built our cabin just about an hour and a half north of our home. We wanted to be close enough to enjoy it often yet far enough away to allow us to fully appreciate the remote and isolated nature. We purchased the land in 2007, began building in 2013, and completed our weekend getaway spot roughly a year later. The winding road we now know so well delivers us almost weekly to our cabin where we indulge in both quiet time together and solitary endeavors. For me, for about a third of the year, those solitary hours mean one thing: snow.

When we arrive at the cabin after a big snow, the chores begin. First, the long driveway needs to be cleared. But the trick here is that the snowblower is kept in the garage—at the end of the driveway.

Tracy has the pleasure of watching from the warmth of the car as I high-step through the deep snow, making my way to the garage. With the snowblower up and running, I blow a path back to the car and one to the house to free Tracy. Once that's done, I have the task of clearing the rest of the driveway to pull the car in.

My chores don't end there. Solar panels are a wonderful invention for powering a cabin tucked away in the remote Idaho woods.

The thing is they need sun to function. So, more time is spent clearing the panels.

While it seems like a lot of work to be done for a weekend's enjoyment, the payoff is worth it. I love the opportunity to get out into the vast stillness that is southwestern Idaho covered in snow. There is really nothing quite like it.

But all that blinding, isolated quiet gives you a lot of time alone with your thoughts. Friday, February 19, my thoughts were consumed by my daughter and her impending trip.

I try my best to remain "hands off" in these situations with my children. After all, they are adults, impossible though that still seems to me at times. Sometimes, I'll admit, Hanna doesn't make that easy.

As I worked my way through the snow that Friday evening, I reflected on Hanna's relative silence since her arrival in the Netherlands for a short visit with friends and family before heading on to Egypt.

After nine months with her mother and me at home, she leaves for Amsterdam and drops off the face of the Earth.

This always happens when she goes to Amsterdam. It swallows her up, and we don't hear from her for days at a time. That is not unusual, but during Hanna's time at home during the COVID pandemic, I'd grown accustomed to our conversations, and I don't think I had been fully prepared for them to end so abruptly once she traveled to Amsterdam.

I'm not being sentimental here—I'm thinking specifically about our talks regarding her upcoming trip. When Hanna first told us about her plans to travel to Egypt and live there for a year, I, of course, had questions. She planned to fulfill a dream of becoming a "digital nomad," as her job as a digital marketing specialist and web analyst gave her the freedom to work from anywhere, but I was wondering if she'd fully thought it through.

You see, Hanna is a dreamer, which is a wonderful thing to be. She is constantly exposing her mother and me to new things—new foods, new experiences, new ideas. We're better people for it. But she'll follow a dream on a whim, and as her father, it's my job to try to look down the road to see just where that whim might take her. I try not to badger. I resist the urge to say, "No, you're not doing that." Mostly, I ask questions and let her reach her own conclusions.

There's something I've learned raising children—particularly, raising daughters—that I try to impart on other new fathers as they begin their journeys into parenthood. You will never win an argument. Don't even try. In fact, the moment it goes from a conversation to an argument you are trying to win, you've already lost. This was never more apparent to me than when our daughters were teenagers.

The job of a teenager—their whole purpose—is to become independent. They are in a weird time where they are beginning to separate from you and forge their own path into adulthood. It's evolutionary. Everything inside of them is screaming to separate, to try things their way. And because of that, you will never win an argument with a teenager. The moment you use your power as a parent to win an argument, you become threatening, and they will never hear a word you have to say.

So, my advice is to make your point, make it in a calm voice, and be direct. Offer your view, and if you can't be calm, walk away. If you do that, nine times out of ten, they will hear you, and your advice will have a much bigger impact. They won't admit it, of course. They'll insist you're old fashioned, and you don't get it, but if you make your point with love, it will get through in the end.

Those early years of learning to navigate our boundaries have paid off as my children have grown into adults. We've all settled into the roles we play in any conversation, and though I'm sure my direct approach still frustrates them at times, we all know how the conversation is going to go. They present an idea, and I challenge them to look at it from a different angle.

Sometimes, I'll admit, I'm maybe a bit too direct, and I know I still say things they don't want to hear. When your adult daughter tells you out of nowhere that she's moving to Egypt for a year, pointed questions about whether she's considered all the horrifying ways her plans could go wrong probably aren't high on the list of responses she's hoping to receive.

Still, we didn't argue over it. I didn't say, "It's a dumb idea—you shouldn't go." Maybe I should have. But what I did do was try to open her mind to my concerns. As long as she knew what they were, maybe she'd have better luck avoiding them turning into realities.

In the days, weeks, and months leading up to her departure, Hanna and I had many of these conversations. Hanna is well-traveled, having grown up in an international family. She's smart and can take care of herself. Still, there are corners of the world where things work a bit differently. This was my biggest reservation as her father.

Hanna had been to Egypt before on vacation with her now ex-boyfriend, who was Egyptian. I couldn't help but wonder if the lens Hanna had seen Egypt through on that brief trip was a bit rose-tinted.

This trip would be different. In fact, it wouldn't be a trip at all. Since she'd be staying there for a year, she'd be more immersed in the culture and would settle into day-to-day life, well off the beaten tourist path. While she saw the excitement in this, I could only seem to see the danger.

I also knew that a pretty, blonde, well-off white woman traveling to Egypt with an Egyptian boyfriend looked a lot different to locals than that same woman arriving alone and attempting to make it her home. Would the wrong person see her day after day and pick up on her routines after noticing she was by herself? Would someone peg her as an easy target for a high ransom?

When I posed these questions to my daughter, I could see the wall go up. Hanna would divert her attention elsewhere, give a short response—"I've been to Egypt. I travel all the time. I know how to take care of myself"—and I'd see her mentally wave me off. *Dad's being close-minded again.* As if I didn't know what the world could be like. As if these things don't happen every day.

They could never happen to *her*. That's how she saw it. And I worried that very belief would put her in danger of being proven wrong.

These were the conversations and thoughts that kept parading through my mind that Friday night as I worked my way through the snow.

But Hanna would be fine. That's what I told myself. I kept clearing that snow and trying to clear my head.

Later that night, we received her message as we were preparing for bed.

Next chapter begins today!

There she was after all those months of planning and discussion, teetering on the edge, about to go over, dive in. I pictured her at the airport, about to scan her ticket and board the plane that would take her even further out of reach.

The thought conjured up a moment in my mind. A handful of months back, we'd been out hiking Toxaway Loop, a scenic but rigorous trail through the Sawtooth Mountains. Locals and tourists alike describe the hike as nothing short of a dream, as it weaves through the mountain peaks and meanders past not one but several crystal blue alpine lakes.

Even though summer was coming to a close and the day was hot, those waters promised to be breathtakingly cool. Before we even set out for the day, Hanna announced her determination to jump in. I had no such intentions. As warm as the day might shape up to be, I knew those lakes would be frigid.

When we arrived at the first lake, Hanna dunked her fingertips in and tested the waters. I could see it instantly on her face: cold.

"I think I'll wait until the next lake," she decided, standing up and wiping her hands on her pants. "We've still got a lot of ground to cover."

I shot a knowing smile at my stubborn daughter. "You know, you don't have to swim today," I offered playfully. "No one is keeping score."

She shot back a look that I know well. "I'm going to swim today," she declared, and I knew in that moment that she would. That's Hanna. She'd made up her mind, and once she'd spoken the words out loud, there was no going back.

"The next lake might be even colder," I cautioned. It is a father's duty to present all the facts, after all.

"And it'll be later in the day—warmer," she retorted as she gathered her things and took off down the trail ahead.

I did my best to tamp down my grin and followed after her.

By the time we reached Toxaway Lake, the sun was high, and Hanna had proved herself right. It was warmer—hot, even—and the heaviness of our packs combined with the fact that we had seriously underestimated the length of the route meant we were both in need of some refreshment—though mine would come in the form of drinking it, not diving into it.

Hanna dropped her pack and immediately began peeling off her shoes and socks. Just looking at the water, though, I could tell I had been right as well. It looked beautiful and inviting—but cold.

I had half a mind to protest. *It's going to be too cold. I wouldn't jump in if I were you.* But I knew there'd be no point. She'd made up her mind. Snow could be falling from the sky, and Hanna's pride and determination would have her in that lake anyway.

Besides, I didn't have the time to say a word. Nearly as soon as she had dropped her shoes on the rocky shore, there she was, diving in.

"How is it?" I called to her as she swam further out into the lake.

She laughed and turned back to face me. She was visibly shivering but had a satisfied smile plastered to her face. "Cold!" she shouted. It wasn't an admittance of defeat though. *You were right, Dad. But so was I. I can take care of myself.*

The memory, months old but still fresh in my mind, buoyed me momentarily as I stared at her message.

`Next chapter begins today!`

I read it again and considered my response: *Be aware of your surroundings. Remember to use your American passport.* Was there something else I had forgotten to mention? My fingers hovered over my phone screen. What wisdom could I cram into these final moments before she dove in—boarded the plane?

Before I could type a response, Tracy beat me to it. Her message bubbled up in our group chat.

It was a photo Tracy had snapped earlier that night of the cabin covered in deep, Idaho snow with the accompanying caption: `Safe travels, our love! You're missing all the snow!`

Safe travels. What more was there to say? A wish, a prayer, an instruction all in one.

We climbed into bed. Sleep was sure to come swiftly as my aching body settled in after hours and hours of snow removal. I don't remember whether we talked about Hanna as we drifted off.

We were asleep when the next message came sometime in the middle of the night.

`I think I'm good on the snow for now. I'm ready for some sun.`

SATURDAY, FEBRUARY 20ᵀᴴ

TRACY

Parenting is an exercise in faith. From the moment your children are born, you are tasked with an objective singular and clear: keep them safe. Other things too, yes. Keep them fed, keep them warm, keep them happy, be there when they need to talk. But above all else, keep them safe.

And for the first few years, after you get past the utter shock that someone let you walk right out of the hospital suddenly with this tiny human being in your care, and your care alone, you find that, overall, there's so much you can control. What they eat, what they wear, where they go, who they interact with. It's all up to you. The urge to have tabs on them at all times is so ingrained in you, you can identify their cry across a crowded playground, determine from the first signs of a runny nose whether this is going to be a quickly passing cold or something more.

You hold their wriggling hands at the road's edge, provide the safety net of your open arms as they climb the ladder to the slide, cut their food into tiny bites appropriate for tiny mouths, and wait by the door with coat, gloves, and hat to protect them from the cold on a snowy day. Their entire existence is tethered to your every "yes," "no," "not right now," "ask me again later."

But as time goes by, you're asked to slowly relinquish that control you've been conditioned to grasp tight. You hear "I can do it myself" more than "Mommy, can you help me?" There are requests (often demands) for space, for privacy. Bit by bit, they break free until, one day, they are grown and out of your hands entirely. On that day, all you can do is place them into God's and pray. Pray that you equipped them well enough to care for themselves the way you have cared for them from the moment they drew their first breath. And have faith.

That Saturday morning, the first thing I did was reach for my phone on the bedside table. I'd messaged with Hanna briefly the night before as she prepared to board her plane in Amsterdam. We knew she had had a connecting flight, but by now, she should have landed in Aghasour, a town in Egypt she planned to explore before settling in for her year abroad.

I think I'm good on the snow for now. I'm ready for some sun.

That was the last message she had sent, sometime after Jon and I had gone to bed.

A bit dismayed that there had been no update since, I sat for a moment on the bed to collect my thoughts. *Speaking of snow*, I thought as I gazed out the window into the drifts that surrounded the cabin, blinding in the early morning light.

Since I'm a fourth-generation Idahoan, one might assume that I am just as eager as Jon to get out into the snow, but I'd rather take advantage of the peace that comes with the falling flakes and admire the quiet beauty from behind the windows of our cozy weekend cabin. Snow is *not* my thing. Actually, *cold* is not my thing, and where there is snow, you can pretty much count on finding cold as well.

Once Jon carves that first path from the car to the front door, I'm content to stay inside. I had plenty to keep me busy that weekend, but I knew my mind would be occupied by thoughts of Hanna. Until she finally checked in, I'd wonder.

I said parenting is an exercise in faith. I did not say that you're well-versed in it by the time your children are thirty years old and traveling alone across the world.

On the other side of the bed, I felt Jon stir. Looking over, I saw that he too had reached for his phone first thing. He'd be looking for a message letting us know she'd arrived safely: *Picked up my bags! Egypt, I've arrived!*

I watched as he opened the app and checked our group chat, then waited as he read and processed her last message. I could nearly see him doing the math in his head as he calculated the hours. A subtle frown darkened his features as he determined we were, in fact, past due for a check-in of that nature. I could see him visibly shake it off and set the phone aside. He didn't say a word. He didn't have to.

That's Hanna.

Hanna moved home during the COVID quarantine months. There, the three of us lived, ate, slept, and worked—remotely—practically side by side for nine months. Jon and Hanna were both working full time, and I, having retired earlier that year from my public position, still had plenty of work to do for various boards and committees I sat on. I also quite literally remodeled the house around them.

In my defense, they weren't originally supposed to be home during work hours. It had been years since Hanna had lived with us, and having her there was a welcome change. When Hanna is away, she is very much an independent woman. We might not hear from her for days—maybe even weeks—at a time if we don't check in with her first. But when Hanna is home, Hanna is *home*.

We sometimes joke about how she's a lot like her cat—a cat we were tasked with caring for during her absence. During those months, while working in my office, I'd often look up to find she had silently settled on the couch across from me with her laptop just to be in the presence of another warm body. Sometimes, if she was feeling chatty, she'd follow me from room to room, excitedly rambling on about her life plans. She'd pop into my bedroom to say she was making tea—would I like a cup? Even during her more solitary, quieter moments, if I were to come into her room while she was watching a movie, for example, she'd pull back the covers and make space for me to join without saying a word.

Hanna has always craved and sought out that connection and companionship. I suppose that's what keeps her heart wandering across the globe, bouncing from place to place, searching for connection.

That said, when Hanna is checked out of Hotel Willems, she *is checked out.* Since she had departed a few weeks earlier—enjoying an extended stopover in Amsterdam to spend time with her sister, Taylor, and friends before heading to Egypt—I think I'd tricked myself into thinking she would be more communicative than she had been before her lengthy stay at home.

In hindsight, I think part of that was likely because we still had her cat. Before Hanna came to stay with us, it'd been years since we'd had a pet in the house. Nonetheless, I was happy to take on the responsibility—I appreciated that cat for the tiny thread of connection to my daughter she represented.

I imagined her then, just hours into her adventure, fully immersed in her new Egyptian life. Savoring her first meal, exploring a local market, engaging wholeheartedly with everyone she met— each stranger now an opportunity to build that bond, grasp a sense of community in her new home. Maybe she was toasting to the excitement ahead at that very moment, a glass of something bubbly in her hand, that infectious smile spread across her face.

I tried to smile then too, tried to hold on to the genuine excitement I held for her and let go of the sting that I had felt for months listening to her planning, and during the hours I'd spent helping her pack. I hoped she was holding on to all the advice her dad and I had provided her as well as last night's wish of "safe travels" in my last message.

Checking my phone one more time, I decided that was enough speculation for now. I shook the thoughts from my mind and rose from the bed to get on with my day, one nagging notion hanging on by a thread.

She could have at least texted when she landed.

JON

That day, I went out on my snowmobile. Surrounded by nothing but fresh air and all that powdery white, I was able to enjoy a solitude I hadn't experienced in some time. It felt like a tiny reset, the way weekend recreations often feel like a brief refueling of the mind and spirit before you return to the grind of the workweek. So quiet, so alone, you can hear your own heartbeat. The world could be ending somewhere out in civilization, and I wouldn't have a clue unless a meteor fell from the sky and landed at my feet. There's so much distraction in this world, sometimes it's good to disconnect. Out there, I'm disconnected. Unreachable.

Well, I would have been unreachable if it weren't for Tracy. For Christmas, Tracy had gotten me a satellite phone. After one too many times getting stuck in the snow, one too many underestimated hikes, she'd finally gotten tired of not being able to reach me. Some might call Tracy a worrier, but to be fair, you cannot label someone a worrier if you are constantly giving them reasons to worry. And Lord knows our family is good at that.

That morning, before heading out on my snowmobile, I had set up my new satellite phone. *There.* I was now reachable wherever, whenever.

"Got your phone?" Tracy had called to me as I'd piled on the cold weather gear, preparing to head out the door.

I'd pulled the device from my pocket and waved it wordlessly in demonstration. *Got it.*

Later, as I stared out over the never-ending blanket of white ahead of me, the world so still I was sure a sudden clearing of my throat could send snow tumbling down the mountainside and birds scattering from the trees, I couldn't help but wonder if having the phone on me cheapened it a bit. There was something about being completely disconnected from everyone and everything. Totally alone.

It was not lost on me that many people around the world were tired of being alone by this point, some having been cooped up in their apartments for months during quarantine without the physical presence of another human. But as I had been living in the construction zone we call a home with my wife, grown daughter, *and* her cat, the seclusion on the mountain that day was a welcome relief.

Still, I knew having that phone in my pocket gave Tracy one less thing to be concerned about. She could reach me if she needed to.

But I knew it wasn't me she was worried about reaching at the moment.

When I'd woken that morning to discover no check-in from Hanna, I admit I was a bit dismayed, but I wasn't surprised. Still, I knew it would be on Tracy's mind. Nevertheless, we went about our morning routines as usual. That's the thing about parenthood that no one really tells you. Of course, you worry about your children. All the time. It's only natural. But if you let that worry control your every waking thought until it is resolved, it will consume you.

I think about this a lot in terms of coaching. When the kids were younger, I took the opportunity to share my love of soccer with them and signed up to be their coach. When they're real little, it can be absolute chaos. They're running all over the field, sometimes in the wrong direction. This one is over here kicking the ball toward the other team's goal; that one is over there picking a dandelion.

But as frustrating as it may be to watch as the kids run about like a bunch of feral cats on the field, it's still their game. You're the coach. You want to run out onto the field and grab them by the hands, place them in the correct spots, tell them when and how hard to go after the ball, but it's the kids' game. The moment you get too involved, it becomes about you.

In life, just as in soccer, you do your best to prepare them with the skills they need to do things on their own. You practice, you coach, then you send them onto the field and trust that they're going to recall everything you taught them while they're out on their own.

Sure, I'd have loved a call or message from Hanna to tell us she'd landed safely, expertly executed that game plan we'd discussed so many times. But mostly, I tried to figure no news was good news. She was off playing her game. I just couldn't see her from my current vantage point on the sidelines.

Cruising through the snow, the crisp air scraping my exposed cheeks, I sighed. It felt good to be present in the moment. But that day, I kept getting stuck. Every time I broke myself free, a few minutes later, I'd find myself dug in again in deep layers of fresh powder. It was growing increasingly frustrating. As soon as I thought I was in the clear, I'd find myself waist deep in a snow drift with five hundred pounds of snowmobile to break free.

I had no idea how much I'd soon wish this was the worst of my problems.

TRACY

When Jon left to go snowmobiling, I was busy on my phone doing some board work and trying to find recipes for the latest diet kick Hanna had somehow convinced me to try with her.

"It may be winter in Idaho, but you'll be on a beach in Mexico before you know it," she had reminded me recently.

"Well, okay," I'd conceded. Every time Hanna proposed something like this—whether it was a new meal plan, an exercise program, or a much more relaxing activity, like an evening at home with facials and pizza—I was eager to agree to whatever it was. I know how lucky I am to have a daughter Hanna's age who actually wants to share interests with her mother. I treasure that deeply.

Hanna has a knack for always pulling us into her adventures in one way or another. Months back, a week before Thanksgiving, I had answered a call from an ecstatic Hanna. I could practically feel her buzzing on the other end of the line. I'm familiar with this energy and stopped what I was doing, preparing for her to present her case. I could tell an ask or major announcement of some sort was coming.

Then, too, she had been multiple flights and several hours away on an impromptu trip to Kauai with my son—her older brother—and his family. They were scheduled to return home in a day or two, but I could tell just from her tone that she was not in the frame of mind of someone whose vacation was about to come to a close. *Here we go,* I thought.

At that point, she had recently come home from her first trip to Egypt. No sooner had her plane touched down on American soil than she had told us she intended to return—and to stay in Egypt. Now, here I was thinking I was about to hear that, *actually*, it was Kauai that had captured her heart, and could I please pack up her things and Kaya—her cat—and get them on a plane?

If I'm being honest, Kauai would have been a welcome change of plans over Egypt. No matter how much I supported my daughter's plans outwardly, I hadn't yet fully wrapped my brain around them.

But no, it turned out Hanna was not, in fact, planning a move to Kauai. She *was* planning something though. And that something happened to involve her dad and me joining her for a festive Hawaiian Thanksgiving.

If there's one thing to know about Hanna, it's that her enthusiasm is nothing short of infectious. She can make the most harebrained ideas seem like the opportunity of a lifetime, not to be missed! I remember shaking my head in amusement with just a smidge of disbelief as I listened to her go on and on about her plans.

"Please, please, please, Mom. It'll be so much fun!" she begged. I could hear the waves crashing in the background.

I still can't believe how I scrambled to make the arrangements, how we dropped everything for Thanksgiving with Hanna in Hawaii. I suppose I can though, really. Because, true to many of the adventures Hanna has roped us into, she had been right. Far from being traditional, our candlelit Thanksgiving dinner in the tropical breeze as we watched the moon rise high above the Pacific Ocean was nothing short of magical. That's the other thing about Hanna: her enthusiasm is so infectious because it comes from a place of true, genuine love and wanting to share the beauty she finds in the world with those she cares for.

My thoughts were interrupted when my phone pinged in my hand. A message from my sister asking if I wanted to work out together—one way we stay connected even when we're apart. No word from Hanna. I wondered how long it would be before we got the call that begged us to join her, as she was dying to show us around her new home.

I was, of course, already planning our trip to visit her. I had been looking at tickets and planning the sights we'd want to see in Cairo and the surrounding areas. But in truth, I could wait a little longer to receive that particular text. Jon and I were planning another vacation at the moment—our anniversary trip to Cancun.

Sitting in front of the fire with snow glistening outside the windows, I couldn't believe that in just over a week, we'd be boarding a plane ourselves, bound for sun and sand and celebration. It would be good to get away. By that time, Hanna would have been settled in her new home, and with any luck, this unease and apprehension that seemed to surround her travels would have subsided.

Opening a browser on my phone, I navigated to the webpage for the resort we'd be staying at. With the Idaho chill in my bones and a million thoughts on my mind, I searched for a distraction. Daydreaming about the warmth of the sun and an itinerary filled with swimming, walking along the beach, and relaxing seemed like a good use of my time. I scrolled past pictures of the many pools and the white sand on the beaches. For a moment, my mind was at ease, somewhere far away, lounging on a beach.

After some time, I clicked back over to our group chat.

I think I'm good on the snow for now. I'm ready for some sun.

Making up my mind, I typed out a reply.

Me too! Cancun, here we come!

I hit send and waited a moment. One gray tick. The message had sent. At least I knew our internet was working. A moment later: two gray ticks. Message successfully delivered.

I'm not sure how long I waited, hoping to see those two blue ticks that would indicate Hanna had read the message. Then, I realized those ticks wouldn't turn blue until Jon had read it too, and he was out somewhere deep in the woods. *Hopefully, he's enjoying himself,* I thought a bit begrudgingly. He certainly wasn't sitting here holding his breath for a message.

My phone buzzed while I held it in my hand. Again, it was Lesly, my sister.

Have time now?

I breathed a deep sigh. Of course, I had time.

SUNDAY, FEBRUARY 21ST

JON

Sunday morning, I awoke with a start. I had slept long and hard, pouring myself into bed at the end of the long, cold day and thawing out as the heat from the fireplace seeped into my sore muscles. But that morning, as my eyes opened and adjusted to the sunlight streaming in through the windows, there was something tugging at the back of my mind. Like the feeling when you wake up in the morning knowing you have an urgent work task to attend to first thing.

Instinctively, I reached for my phone. I knew it would be there. Hanna would have finally messaged, and we would be able to breathe a sigh of relief, shake our heads over Hanna's absentmindedness while sipping our morning coffee, and get back to enjoying the rest of our weekend. I was eager to get on with it.

Except there was no message. I opened the app and the group chat Tracy, Hanna, and I shared just to be sure. Nothing. Only then did I register that Tracy was already awake beside me, sitting up in bed.

The previous night, over dinner and a bottle of wine, we had not talked about Hanna. In fact, neither of us had mentioned her all day. That, in itself, should have been the warning sign that worry was starting to root in our minds. Normally, we would have wondered aloud to each other how she was doing, speculated on the progress of her trip, probably even voiced minor frustrations about how she hadn't checked in. The fact that neither of us had so much as mentioned her name spoke volumes.

At first, I hadn't brought it up because Tracy hadn't brought it up. If Tracy was distracted enough to not have registered the lack of communication as a concern, I certainly wasn't going to be the one to make her wonder if it should be. Then, I had returned from my afternoon of somewhat less than leisurely snowmobiling—after digging myself out half a dozen times—and I'd seen Tracy's message in our group chat. I'll admit to the momentary flush of relief I had felt when, upon stepping into the warmth of the cabin and pulling my cell phone out of my pocket, I saw the notification of a message received.

I could hear the shower running—Tracy must have done a workout with Lesly while I was out—and in the stillness of the cabin, I allowed myself to pause and take a deep breath before opening the message as snow dripped from my boots onto the mat beneath my feet.

At that point, I think I still felt that everything was fine. I wanted a resolution to this quiet, wanted to be able to greet Tracy with a hot cup of tea when she emerged from the shower and casually say, "Did you see Hanna finally checked in?" But when I opened the message, I saw Tracy had only responded to Hanna's earlier message at some point in the afternoon.

Me too! Cancun, here we come!

Taking in the lightheartedness of my wife's message, I thought for a moment that maybe it was all in my mind. Maybe I was the one worrying unnecessarily for once.

But as the day wore on, I still couldn't bring myself to mention Hanna.

Then, Sunday morning, as Tracy sat next to me in bed, looking at her phone with a frown, the silence of not speaking Hanna's name felt like a heaviness in the air that could burst at any moment. I decided to take a pin to it before it came crashing down at a later, unexpected moment.

"She hasn't been messaging you separately?" I asked, breaking the silence of the room.

She looked across the bed at me. A small shake of her head.

"You?" she asked.

"No."

We sat there in strangely companionable silence. The cat was out of the bag, and it was somehow both better and worse. It was a relief to know we weren't alone in our concerns, but suddenly, it felt a little more real. Neither of us was waving it off and saying, "You're worrying over nothing. You'll see. It's just Hanna being Hanna."

We did talk about it then. I remember that. But I could tell we were both still being careful around the subject, neither of us voicing our deepest concerns.

"My biggest fear, Hanna, is that someone will figure out who you are, learn about our family. They'll kidnap you and ask for a ransom—which we'll pay. Of course, we'll pay. They'll ask for more and more. They'll bleed us dry, and your head will still come back in a box."

It had been one of our more heated discussions about her decision to move to Egypt. We were at the cabin for the weekend shortly before she left for Amsterdam. We were out for a short hike through the property, just the two of us, and I was revisiting all of the best points I'd made over the previous months, making sure they were drilled in.

Then, I had stopped suddenly, breathless from trudging through hardened snow, and blurted this out. Maybe not my best exercise at staying calm, but I was growing concerned that I hadn't been blunt enough with my daughter to make her truly understand my fears.

I remember she too had stopped then and just stared silently ahead, but there was something there. A flicker in her eyes. I couldn't tell if I had finally cracked the surface of something—was it fear? Had I finally sparked even just a hint of unease about what she was getting herself into? Or was it something else? Disappointment in a perceived lack of confidence in her?

"I know, Dad. I know."

The air felt wrong after that. Like I'd dropped a glass at a party, and the cadence of the festivities could never quite get back to normal. As we walked back toward the cabin, where Tracy was waiting with a hot meal on the table, the distance between us steadily grew until we were each walking on our own. When Hanna had nearly reached the cabin ahead of me, I could see her slow her pace. I picked up my own just a bit, and we walked in together, though neither of us spoke about what had been said.

Over dinner that night, we sipped wine while Tracy and Hanna talked excitedly about her plans to dive in the Red Sea and take part in efforts to clean up the beaches and the coral reefs. Her eyes flickered again but not with fear or disappointment. In the glow of the candlelight, all I could see was strength, determination, unrelenting optimism.

She wouldn't understand until she one day had a daughter of her own that as her father, my biggest fear was that someone else would see those same things and want to extinguish them. I remember hoping in that moment that I was being as needlessly overprotective as she thought I was being.

Tracy got up to grab something from the kitchen, and there was a brief silence as Hanna and I sat at the table alone. Finally, she looked across at me and spoke.

"I've been listening, you know."

I didn't know what to say in reply, so I waited until she spoke again. She gave a small, reassuring smile and nodded her head before continuing.

"I have. And I've heard you."

Tracy returned to the table then. Sitting down and pulling her chair in, she raised her wine glass.

"We should have a toast!" she declared, beaming at Hanna, who was still looking at me as we too raised our glasses.

"To our adventurous girl," Tracy began. "To chasing dreams and following a calling. And to new adventures!"

"Proost!"

TRACY

We've never been a big churchgoing family, but I find a Sunday morning out in the cool mountain air can be just as spiritually refreshing as any church service. That Sunday, Jon and I ventured out of the cabin together.

Now, I've said it before, and I'll say it again—I'm not a snow person. Sign me up for a bike ride or hike any season of the year, but if there's snow on the ground, light me a fire and put a good book in my hands. I'll gladly appreciate the snow's beauty from behind the glass.

I do, however, enjoy snowshoeing. That is one winter activity I can layer on the snow pants, boots, gloves, and hat for. There is just something about the stillness of the Idaho wilderness under a fresh layer of untouched snow that invites the calm that is needed for internal reflection and for listening. Listening for the messages you might have missed in the hustle and bustle of daily life.

As we trekked through the snow, we enjoyed the quiet of the landscape around us. The only sounds were the occasional chirp of a winter bird and the sound of our own breathing as we made our way across the otherwise empty land. Those plus the thumping of my heart in my chest and the thoughts racing through my mind.

Still, there was something about having cleared the air, about knowing Jon and I were on the same page, that gave me some comfort. It wasn't the comfort of knowing everything would be okay—I've been through enough as a parent to know there's always something else coming over the next hill—but rather the comfort of knowing that whatever our family would face, we would face it together. We never carry these things on our own.

Perhaps this is the benefit of hindsight, but something was off in the air that day. It was too calm. Too still. As if the world—as if God—were giving us a moment. A moment to brace ourselves and to catch our breath. You never know the true meaning of the calm before the storm until you experience it for yourself.

JON

That morning, before Tracy and I left the cabin, our snowshoes in tow, I resolved to send a message to Hanna. We don't like to meddle or come across as the untrusting parents all children are apt to view their parents as at some point. However, the more the hours ticked by, the sillier it seemed that we hadn't just taken the initiative to put an end to our own wondering.

Hi, Hanna! Are you safe and well in Egypt? Please check in when you can. We've been waiting to hear from you.

Before hitting send, I thought better of it and deleted the last two lines.

Hi, Hanna! Are you safe and well in Egypt?

There. It was sent, and soon enough, we'd hear back and be able to move on from all the "what ifs" that had been running through our minds all weekend.

Perhaps not wanting to watch the proverbial pot as we waited for it to boil, we headed out into the winter sun and out of cell phone service.

Still, our trek that morning didn't have the usual lightness of the quiet moments we reserve to connect with each other. Everything around us felt loaded, and an almost overwhelming sense of foreboding hung in the air.

By the time we returned in the early afternoon and checked our phones—once again to find nothing—the worry had taken on an almost physical quality in the atmosphere of the cabin. As we went about our day, our thoughts crept more and more into our conversations. We volleyed "what ifs" and "probably justs" back and forth.

In the evening, we bundled up and enjoyed a Dutch salad and a glass of wine on the patio under the heaters. Who could remember now what we talked about on that evening just hours before everything changed? We snapped a couple of happy photos, glasses raised, coats buttoned tight against the cold air, and Tracy probably filled me in on the plans she had been making for our anniversary trip. But I'm sure our thoughts and conversation kept drifting back to our daughter. Still, we enjoyed the evening as best we could.

As the sun went down and the moon rose above the cabin, we settled into another stretch of silence—this time, a more comfortable one. I remember reaching over and squeezing Tracy's hand as we both gazed up at the sky. The moon that night was roughly two-thirds full. If Hanna had been there, she'd have been able to tell us whether it was waxing or waning—could probably have even offered some insight into how it was affecting our current dispositions.

I don't think either of us really wanted to go to bed. By ten o'clock our time, it was early morning in Aghasour. I think we both wanted to give Hanna some time to wake up, give ourselves a chance at receiving her reply before we turned in for a night of what would otherwise be restless sleep.

We didn't need to wait long for an excuse to stay awake. Just as we were slowly preparing to give up and turn in, it came. Not the text we were waiting for but a particularly unwelcome distraction.

The roof above our heads, bearing the weight of literal tons of snow, had begun to leak.

TRACY

Just a few days before Hanna departed from Amsterdam, finally on her way to Egypt, I received an unexpected call from my daughter. Like I've said, it is often rather unusual to hear from Hanna when she's back in Amsterdam and fully immersed in all it has to offer—everything from old friendships to the vibrant nightlife we've never seemed to entirely understand the allure of.

Part of me had a feeling she'd be even more out of touch once she officially landed in Egypt. So, when she called out of the blue one evening (her time), I was happy to soak in those precious moments when she'd thought to call and hear my voice rather than just text.

Again, she was buzzing, clearly excited about something.

"I'm here with Mia and Niels, Mom. Niels has never heard the song! Mom, you have to sing him the song."

Mia and Niels, two of Hanna's closest friends, were expecting their first child. The song—I quickly caught on through Hanna's energetic insistence that I sing it over the phone to her friends—was a song Hanna had loved for as long as I could remember. As much as I've always considered it to be "our song" since she was a baby, it truly is Hanna's song.

So, I introduced Niels to the song Hanna hoped he would sing one day soon to his new baby, just as I had sung it to her. And while I sang, my heart was warmed because Hanna thought to include me in that special moment from across the world. I pictured her, my grown baby girl, sitting under the moon in Amsterdam as the lyrics traveled down the line.

I see the moon,
and the moon sees me.
The moon sees the one I long to see.
God bless the moon,
and God bless me.
And God bless the one I long to see.

Hanna's journey to faith has been a bit of a winding road. Just like us all, Hanna is still traveling that road, and I imagine she will continue to do so as her life presents further trials and obstacles to navigate around. I think those of us who are further along in our walks often forget that you sometimes have to go the long way around to reach your destination. And Hanna is still young.

Still, Hanna has always had a spiritual side.

She's always felt a deep spiritual connection to the moon, a connection we could see in her even as a small child. We'd sing our lullaby often, and she'd sit at her window, staring up at the moon in the sky. It was evident that she drew comfort and inspiration from its very presence, and isn't that what faith is all about anyway? I was glad to be a part of this and to nurture her growing spirituality.

In the cabin that night, I could hear Jon above me on the roof, shoveling the snow to the ground below, each shovelful landing with a dull thud. A leak in your roof on a winter's night is something that tends to demand your immediate attention, but after I had appropriately placed the buckets and laid out the towels, I found myself standing at the window, staring up at the moon.

I sent up a silent prayer for everyone I loved underneath it— from my husband out on the slick roof to my kids and their families nearby, likely tucked safely into bed, to Taylor in Amsterdam, rising now to start her day, and to Hanna, the one I suddenly longed to see more than ever before.

I realized that Hanna could have easily recited that song to her friends herself, and standing at the window in the cabin, I felt a wave of gratitude wash over me. I couldn't have known then just how tightly I'd hold on to that unexpected phone call from my daughter just days earlier or how many times I'd stare up at that same moon, sending silent prayers out into the night in the weeks to come. But in that moment, I felt a profound tie to my daughter.

And then, the message came.

PART TWO

Over the mountain, over the sea
Back where my heart is longing to be
Please, let the light that shines on me
Shine on the one I love

"I See the Moon," Meredith Willson, 1953

TWO DAYS EARLIER
SATURDAY, FEBRUARY 20TH

HANNA
AGHASOUR, EGYPT

From Hanna's Journal
They took my phone, so I'm writing this on a scrap of paper bag.

———

I landed in Aghasour, Egypt, in the late afternoon after a full day of travel, two flights, and one layover. My gut, though completely empty of actual food, was full of anticipation and the excitement of plans finally coming to fruition. *I am here!*

I couldn't wait to get out of the airport with its stale, recirculated air and bland, prepackaged airport food. I hadn't eaten since Amsterdam, actually. I was looking forward to that first meal on Egyptian soil and figured I'd save myself until I could get out and explore, find something fresh and full of local flavor.

As I made my way to customs, I texted Mia to let her know I'd arrived and Uzair, my business partner, to arrange plans to meet up once I was free of the airport hassle. Customs wouldn't take too long.

I was wrong.

At first, I was just annoyed. The agent who'd examined my passport had raised an eyebrow at my answer when he'd asked my reason for travel. I was traveling for work—sort of. That morning, I'd embarked on the beginning of my year as a digital nomad. The remote nature of my work meant I could go anywhere, *live* anywhere. I chose Egypt first.

After I'd given my answer, the man looked from my face to the passport several times. I noticed then I'd handed him the Dutch one. He was listening, though I sensed he was focused on something else in my voice.

"You're American," he said at last. *Ah. My accent.*

"Yes. Both, actually," I replied, giving a brief explanation of my dual citizenship.

The man nodded, still looking down at my passport as if deciding whether to hand it back. My hand was outstretched, palm open. He looked up but not at me. With another slight nod, he exchanged a look with the agent hovering above my luggage on the low counter to my right.

"Miss," the agent said. "If you would . . ." He gestured with one hand for me to step aside—away from my bags—while the other man began to search my belongings.

As I did, figuring I was the unlucky winner of a random search, the man called back to me.

"Your bag," he said and nodded to my purse slung over my shoulder.

"Of course," I replied, handing it over. I smiled at the man as he reached for it—*look how polite and compliant I am. Can this please be over quickly?*—but the man did not smile back.

All I had on me at that point was my phone. I texted Mia to pass the time.

Getting searched at customs. I added an eye roll emoji for good measure.

Hope they're not health nuts like you, she texted back immediately. *You'll find half your stuff missing.*

That made me laugh. But it triggered something else too. Her joking reference to my "stuff"—mostly vitamins and supplements I'd packed for a year abroad—had tugged at me. A little thread of worry. Something seated deep in my mind or maybe my stomach. Or perhaps it was my intuition.

When I looked up from my phone, I saw that more men— airport security—had gathered around my belongings. They were speaking urgently and emphatically in Arabic, and I couldn't understand a word.

What are they looking at? I couldn't see from where they had me waiting.

The agent who'd initiated this search raised his head in my direction, and his gaze caught mine. He held it. Then, the others looked up. Someone said something, hushed and low. In the back of my mind, that tugging turned into a tiny alarm bell.

Something's not right.

That's what I texted Mia next.

They're taking too long with the search. They've called more people over. Everyone's looking at my bags, and I can't even see what it is they're looking at.

Mia texted back immediately.

You can't see? You mean they're not searching it in front of you?

My stomach dropped. *Of course, they should be searching it in front of me.*

That's when the agent began to walk over. He looked down at the phone in my hand, and I gripped it harder.

"You need to come with me, please." His tone was not impolite, but the "please" did not sound entirely genuine.

The eyes of the other security guards were on me still. They watched, standing over my luggage sprawled out on the table, as I was escorted away. One man was still rifling through my personal items, his hands carelessly pushing things aside. My skin crawled at the thought of what he might be touching, and the idea of leaving all those men there alone with the life I'd packed in a bag for a year of living abroad felt unsettling—violating.

I held on tight to my phone as my feet carried me reluctantly away. Behind me rang a single man's laughter, which was followed by an eruption as the others joined in.

I was deposited in some stuffy back room deep within the airport and told to wait. And wait I did.

For hours, I sat in that room on a hard metal chair, trying to convince myself that I'd be out any minute. I texted with Mia to keep myself calm. I also texted Uzair, whom I was now very late to meet up with. I told him to get dinner without me as my stomach grumbled and growled, and I wished I'd picked up something during my layover.

At one point, I recalled the chewing gum in my purse and, mouth instantly watering at the thought of it, reached around the back of my chair to retrieve it. Of course, it wasn't there. My phone was the only thing they'd left me.

I continued to reassure myself. It was just an unfortunate security check. A minor delay—that's all. What was a few hours when I had a whole year of adventure in Egypt ahead of me?

But more hours passed, and the knots in my stomach tightened.

No one came for me for a long time, and I actually found myself hoping I had simply been forgotten. Someone would come into the room, surprised to find me still sitting there, apologize for the mishap, and send me on my way. But I could hear men talking just outside the door. I couldn't translate what they were saying, but it was clear I hadn't been forgotten.

What are they talking about? Why am I still here? When will somebody just tell me what is going on? The thoughts raced through my mind. I adjusted my stiff body in my seat. Every muscle ached. *Exactly how long have I been sitting here?*

The voices got louder, and I held my breath. I could sense someone standing just on the other side of the door, wrapping up the last of a conversation I couldn't make out. But it had an air of finality to it. *This is almost over,* I told myself.

In that brief moment as the door handle turned, I felt a sudden pang of anxiety at the thought that they might deport me back to Amsterdam for some reason.

The dismay I felt at the idea all but vanished from my mind the moment the door finally opened. A man stepped in, and it was as if all the air in that small, sterile room had been sucked out behind him. This man was different. His authority was palpable.

Through the harsh glow of the fluorescent lights, his eyes were dark, and his cold, fixed expression told me I had worse things to worry about than finding myself back in Amsterdam the next morning. I sat up straight and suddenly in my chair, feeling oddly vulnerable.

My first instinct was to start to bargain like a student in the principal's office realizing they were in for more than a simple detention slip this time. But when I opened my mouth to speak, no words came out. My mouth was dry. I was parched from hours of isolation and no water. And something told me he wasn't there for a discussion.

His hard stare moved from my face downward, landing on my phone still tight within my grasp on the table. The alarm in my head that had been a steady, low hum was now a blaring siren.

"We found drugs. Before we transport you to the police station," he said in heavily accented English, "we need to take your phone."

That's when I felt the bottom drop out.

"What?" I demanded. "Drugs? That's crazy!"

When he didn't respond, I continued. "What drugs? That's just not . . . it's not possible!"

Coldly, he explained they'd found various capsules and bags of powder in my suitcase and a packet of some substance in my purse. He stared me down. I could tell he wanted me to crack.

But what on earth is he talking about? Capsules and pow—

That's when it hit me. The supplements. The protein pancake mix. I actually laughed, though it was devoid of joy and fraught with disbelief.

"Oh, no, no, no," I began. "This is a mistake. Those are just . . . health things. Vitamins. Food, even." I searched his face for some sort of understanding. I found nothing.

And what had they found in my purse? I couldn't even recall what I'd thrown in there now. Could they be talking about gum? Mints? This was ridiculous.

"I need to speak to someone else," I pushed further. "If you'd bring me my bags, I can explain what everything is. If you'd just—"

"Miss," he cut me off. "Your phone." He held out his hand.

The alarm faded into the stillness of my frozen mind. I gripped my phone. He stood there with his palm open expectantly across the table. And instead of complying, I stalled. I texted Uzair.

Something is happening. They are taking me to the police station.

I started deleting messages. I wasn't going to give them any reading material to invent a story from. The battery was a sliver of red. I was buying time I didn't even have.

The man straightened and lowered his arm, clearly aware of what I was doing. He huffed impatiently.

My fingers hovered over two remaining text threads. Mia and . . . my parents. I instantly regretted not texting them that I had landed earlier, back before everything had gotten so out of hand. But what could I say now? I couldn't lie. But I could still get out of this without causing them unnecessary worry.

The guard cleared his throat impatiently, and his body weight shifted from one foot to the other. He was preparing to make a demand. I had just enough time for one last message. I made the decision.

If you don't hear from me in a day or two, tell my parents what happened. Then, I hastily added, *Talk to Uzair!*

Sent. I waited for the message to indicate it had been delivered. *Delete.*

With more reluctance than I've ever experienced in my life, I reached across the table, my phone like an offering in my shaking palm. In an instant, it was snatched away.

SUNDAY, FEBRUARY 21ST
SOMETIME AFTER MIDNIGHT

HANNA
AGHASOUR, EGYPT

From Hanna's Journal
Words cannot describe the immense sorrow and guilt I feel. Words cannot describe the absolute hell I've landed myself in.

How many times did my dad tell me to use my American passport, even when flying from Amsterdam—especially when flying from Amsterdam? And how many times did I secretly roll my eyes in response?

I guess I never imagined this could be the consequence. I look around me now, surrounded by so many women even worse off than I am, and I can't believe how stupid I've been. Privilege is the word sounding in my head now. I've never felt it deeper or sharper than I do right now, worlds away from the reality I've so comfortably taken for granted.

There are moments when my thoughts begin to drift. Suddenly, I'm back on the plane, watching Amsterdam grow smaller and smaller beneath me, the winter moon fading in the daylight. I remember thinking that the next time it rose, I'd be beginning my new life in Egypt. I hold on to that moment for as long as I can.

I'm not sure when I'll see the moon again.

———

When the cell door slammed behind me, I felt my freedom instantly severed, as swift and final as a dropped call before you have the chance to say your goodbyes.

There I was, staring into the blank faces of several women whose sleep had been abruptly disturbed by my arrival. My tired eyes were open wide and burning, unblinking as I rapidly took in my surroundings, attempting to make sense of a situation that was feeling increasingly impossible with every passing second. Women stood leaning against the walls; one had her finger frozen against a patch of peeling paint. More women sat looking up at me from the dirty concrete floor.

The air was sucked from my lungs. I felt I couldn't breathe.

All day, my mind had been reasoning and theorizing, examining my situation and hypothesizing what would happen next. It had been wrong at every turn.

It's just a routine security check. I'll be released any moment. Transport to the police station is just a formality. I'll sit in another sterile room for a couple of hours, then the police will let me go.

Wrong. Recalculate. Wrong. Wrong. Wrong again.

I spun around, my brain refusing to process the scene. Banging on the door, I shouted, "No! There's been a mistake! I need to call my parents!"

I yelled insistently, desperately. No one came.

My breath was coming fast and shallow as the edges of my periphery turned inky black. The room was suddenly and violently turning on its axis, and I had the sensation of tumbling forward with it. I felt sick.

The women were surrounding me now. All attention was on me. They were speaking to me, but everything was a tangled mess of foreign syllables and the sound of my own heart drumming heavily in my ears. Hands were patting me down, stroking my arms and back—a physical attempt to hush and comfort me where words were failing.

All day, I'd held it together. Then, suddenly, I was drowning.

Directly before me, the cluster of women's feet suddenly parted. From somewhere in the back, a woman stepped quietly forward.

"Shhhhh," I heard her whisper. The room fell silent around us.

Slowly, I raised my gaze, palms still firmly planted on my shaking knees. Kind eyes met mine. Deep pools of rich mahogany. I could almost not perceive where her irises stopped and her pupils began.

"Calm," she said, smoothing the fabric of my shirt across my shoulders. An eerie tranquility rushed over me as she placed both hands gently on my shoulders.

"Calm," she repeated.

That one word felt like a hand reaching into the water to pull me out. I took it.

"Speak English?" she asked.

"Yes," I replied, tears still in my voice, but I held on to that word as best I could. *Calm.*

"Safe," she said next. "Understand? Safe."

"No," I felt myself utter breathlessly. "No, this isn't right."

She gave a small, sympathetic smile and took me by the hand, leading me across the crowded cell to a far corner. As we squeezed our way through the bodies of the other women, I found myself stepping over several pairs of legs. It seemed the others were already attempting to go back to sleep.

My anxiety grew with every step away from the door—*I'm not supposed to be here!*—but I followed the woman anyway. Upon looking back, I noted the cell door couldn't have been more than a few paces away from the corner we now stood in. A small bundle of clothes laid at our feet, and the woman gestured for me to sit. I did.

I took her in. Everything about her seemed to match the softness of her eyes. Wispy, dark curls ran along her hairline, just visible under a cream-colored hijab. The hijab itself was discolored in places, darkened where I assumed she lay on her side at night, but her face was clean. Taking in her terracotta skin, I could have sworn this woman was pulled from the clay itself. She filled the tiny space with a warmth and earthiness I cannot describe.

From behind, another woman pressed into me as she made a spot for herself to lie down. I instantly had the regrettable feeling that I was taking up someone else's precious space. Instinctively, I edged myself closer to my new companion.

"You sleep here. Next to me," she said, seeming to pick up on my concern. "Safe."

I shook my head a little. No way I could sleep. Not now. NOT here. *What if they realize this is a mistake? What if someone comes back for me?* But she only nodded back at me.

"Yes," she said. "You sleep. Court soon—maybe tomorrow."

I wasn't sure I could believe her. She nodded again and tried another small, soothing smile.

"You see. Tomorrow, court. For now, you sleep."

A small nod. It was all I could muster. I was tired.

"Now," she began again. "Your shoes." She gestured to the boots I wore on my feet. "Off."

"Oh, no, no, I'm okay," I began to decline. I glanced around. No way could I imagine myself barefoot in here.

"No, see," she cut me off, lifting her bundle of clothes into her lap and unfolding them to reveal a pair of shoes tucked firmly in its center. She wrapped it back up and mimed putting her head on it.

My heart broke for her in that moment. Who has tips and tricks for surviving a night in jail?

Someone who has survived many nights in one, something within me said.

At once, it occurred to me that it might be insulting for me to refuse. *It's just one night,* I told myself as I unlaced my boots.

Moments later, with my head resting on my boots, wrapped loosely in my jacket, and my body squeezed in tightly between two strangers, I inhaled deeply.

My jacket still smelled of home.

SUNDAY, FEBRUARY 21ST TO MONDAY, FEBRUARY 22ND

HANNA

From Hanna's Journal
All there is to pass the time is sleep. And so, I sleep. But even sleep has its limits, and when I wake, here I am again. Still. And for how long? Hours pass. No answers come. No one comes.

Something tickled my nose.

My mind was awake before my eyes, and when I finally opened them, I experienced the momentary sensation of forgetting where I was. Like waking from a nightmare to discover yourself in the safety of your own room, the familiarity of your own bed—but opposite. I'd tumbled from a dream straight into the nightmare of reality.

Shakily, I sat up. A fly buzzed around my head, landing on an eyebrow and making it itch. I swatted it away. The woman from the night before was also awake and clearly had been for some time. She greeted me with that same warm, reassuring smile that had calmed me in my panicked state.

"Hello," she greeted me.

I could only half nod in response. I wasn't awake enough to speak and couldn't yet find my voice. I'd somehow managed to sleep the night before—my jacket wrapped around my boots as a makeshift pillow like she'd taught me—but I didn't feel rested. I began to take in my surroundings, but as my senses started to come back to life—the heat, the smell, the uncanny feeling of the walls closing in around me—something in my mind seized up. *Don't process.*

I looked back at the woman and saw her lips part as she prepared to speak again. It was all too overwhelming. Before she could utter a sound, I turned and lay back down, clutching my bundled boots desperately and squeezing my eyes shut tight.

I don't recall falling asleep. I don't recall much of anything at all.

This continued in a pattern throughout Sunday and well into the small hours of Monday morning. Sleep. Wake. Sleep. Wake. Until at some point, I couldn't sleep any longer. I sat awake and stared up at the ceiling. I counted the flies that darted here and there above me.

It began to feel like the woman's promise from the night I'd arrived had been empty or, at least, misguided. She'd said, "Court tomorrow," hadn't she? It had been late—or early?—when I'd been dumped in the cell, and with all the sleep, it was difficult to tell what time it was or even what day it was.

Losing hope was easy. No one was coming for me. How long had I been waiting?

Out of habit, I kept reaching into my pocket for the phone that wasn't there. Each time I came up empty, something within my chest wound tighter. It felt unnatural and increasingly frustrating, this disconnection from the outside world, but not only that, the sudden inability to do something as simple and mundane as telling the time.

The longer I sat, the more it seemed my thoughts were ricocheting from one corner of my mind to another—*any moment, someone will come and call my name, and I'll be free to go.*

Then, the next minute—*no one is coming for you. No one knows where you are. You are going to be here for a long, long time.*

At one point, I gathered the nerve to go up to the door.

"Excuse me," I called out into the hall. "Excuse me. I need to use the toilet."

Someone tapped me on the shoulder from behind. I turned to find a woman standing there, her arm outstretched toward the far corner of the cell. It took me a moment to realize what she meant to show me. In the air, a collection of flies swirled in a haphazard holding pattern. Below them, a hole in the floor. My stomach turned upside down. Silently, I returned to my spot on the floor. I'd wait. I'd wait to leave. I'd wait until someone came.

The hours passed, and my weary mind wandered. How had I landed myself in this mess? Where had I gone wrong? Had there been a moment to salvage the situation, to right the course? A moment that had somehow slipped through my grasp?

`If you don't hear from me in a day or two, tell my parents what happened.`

I recalled that last text to Mia. I tried to count the hours, blurred and indiscernible between bouts of fitful sleep.

Had it been two days?

"Hanna Willems." The voice sliced through my thoughts. I raised my eyes to see a guard standing, the cell door ajar.

In an instant, I scrambled shakily to my feet, lunging toward the open door.

MONDAY, FEBRUARY 22ND
JUST AFTER MIDNIGHT

JON

I didn't know exactly how long I'd been out on the roof, shoveling the snow to the ground below, trying to find the source of that leak. But the moment I stepped inside, shutting the cold out behind me, I knew something was wrong. Downstairs, I could hear Tracy's voice. Deep in conversation. Serious.

Hanna.

As I rounded the corner and began descending the stairs to the living room, Tracy came into view. Her body language was all wrong. She was rigid and sitting on the very edge of the sofa, phone pressed to her ear. Her expression was wrong too.

Everything about the moment was wrong.

Is it Hanna? I thought, but before I could get the words out of my mouth, my ears actually tuned into what Tracy was saying.

"Taylor, stay calm," she said. "Stay calm, and just tell me what you know."

A step creaked beneath me, and Tracy looked up abruptly. Our eyes met, and I stopped in my tracks.

We drove back from the cabin early the next morning, bleary eyed but with traces of adrenaline coursing through our bloodstreams, keeping us alert. I'd managed some sleep that night. Tracy, I knew, had not.

The relative silence of the past couple of days was now replaced with steady conversation as we made our way down the winding highway toward home, urgent but measured.

What next? What did we know? Arguably, not much.

From the moment I'd joined the conversation, trying to put the pieces together, I'd known it had to be about Hanna. Of course, it did. My mind immediately flipped through the options—*accident? missing? kidnapped?*—in the seconds before it came out: *arrested.* Hanna had been arrested at the airport in Aghasour.

Taylor was in quite the state. In truth, we'd been waiting for that call for days, and then it finally came. What I remember most about it was Taylor's anxiety. Her breathing. It was quick and ragged. I remember our focus somehow shifted and settled on a need to comfort our youngest daughter, to bring her back down to earth as we tried to glean as much information as we could from the call.

Hanna had been detained at customs in the Aghasour airport shortly after she'd arrived. It seemed they had a problem with the supplements she had in her luggage. With some reluctance, Taylor sheepishly admitted that there had—allegedly—been some cocaine in Hanna's possession as well. While they'd been examining her luggage, Hanna had been texting her friend Mia and her business partner, Uzair. But then they'd arrested her. She was able to get a message to Mia that they were taking her to a police station—which one, no one was certain—and that was the last any of them had heard from her.

Mia and her husband, Niels, got the message to Taylor and her boyfriend, Erik. Uzair got in touch with Hanna's ex-boyfriend, Amir. Together, they set to work on a plan. They hired a lawyer—a friend of a friend—and drained their savings accounts to pay his retainer. It totaled 250,000 Egyptian pounds, or around 13,000 euros at the time. That's what they had collectively gathered to pay the fee. All without contacting us first.

Tracy and I couldn't believe what we were hearing.

Next chapter begins today!

I thought about that message from Hanna. While we'd been waiting to hear from her this weekend, it had felt like forever. But now, it seemed impossible that so much had transpired in such a short amount of time without our knowledge. We had just talked to her. And now she was sitting in some Egyptian jail while her friends all banded together and hired a lawyer?

My head was spinning. We were stunned.

"Wait, Taylor, slow down," I interrupted. "Why a lawyer? Why are they holding her in the first place? Are we sure they won't just let her go tomorrow?"

I couldn't wrap my head around it. Something felt off about the whole thing. I mean, it was pancake mix for crying out loud. Cocaine? That could be a problem, of course—if it even was cocaine. With all the vitamins and so on Hanna had taken with her, they could have easily mistaken any one of those items for something it wasn't. Surely, they'd clear it up and just let her go. Turn her around and send her back to Amsterdam, worst case.

"The cocaine—was it even Hanna's?" I asked.

A long pause.

"Dad, I really don't know." She sounded utterly drained. "I really don't know."

While Tracy carried the conversation forward, trying to extract every bit of information Taylor might have forgotten, I worked it over in my mind. They'd searched her bags out of sight. They had what they *thought* was a significant amount of drugs. But we knew it wasn't. And then they had cocaine—supposedly—that had come from where?

"I'm really worried," Taylor confided, her breath still rapid and heavy on the other end of the line. "I have a really bad feeling about this. I don't think they're just going to let her go."

When the sun rose that morning, we found ourselves heading home, clinging to the little information we had.

There had been a brief moment when my initial worst fears were disproven—not in an accident, not missing, not kidnapped and being held somewhere while we waited for a ransom note. But "brief" is the key word there. Arrested. Hanna had been arrested. In Egypt. With the little information we had that Monday morning, *arrested* didn't look much better than the alternatives. We were under no illusions of what being locked away in a foreign country could look like or what consequences Hanna could find herself up against, especially if drugs were suspected.

Where was she being held? What kind of people were holding her? I tried to keep my mind from going to all the dark places it seemed determined to explore.

Is she safe? Is she okay? Oh my God, is she even still alive?

These were the thoughts pressing on us with every mile that passed. These were our top priorities. We needed to get home and get that question answered: *is she safe?* We'd take everything else from there.

How we would answer that question, we had no idea.

HANNA

As I was escorted down the hall, hope welled within my chest. Maybe they wouldn't send me to court after all. Maybe this was it. They'd see my shaken state, the terror on my face, and know they'd accomplished their mission. They'd scared the stupid American girl and could send her on her way, humiliated and dragging her disheveled and pillaged luggage behind her.

While they checked me out at the front desk, I clung desperately to that scenario. *Slap me on the wrist, send me home, give me a giant fine . . . I don't care what it is. Just get me out of here!*

In my gut, I knew it was nothing more than wishful thinking. I wasn't about to walk free. Instead, it was an out of the fire, into the frying pan sort of situation.

I was handcuffed to a guard for transportation, and the feeling of being physically joined to one of my captors almost made me wish I was back in the cell, sandwiched between the other ladies who reeked of desperation and cigarette smoke. All I could smell on the guards was their disdain for me. What'd they see when they looked at me? A spoiled American girl? A would-be drug trafficker? The night I'd arrived, I'd had to beg for a phone call as they walked me down to the cell. It wasn't until I'd shouted the word "embassy" in my pleas that they'd begrudgingly rerouted and given me access to a phone. I was allowed to leave one message with the embassy, then they dumped me into the cell without another word.

In the back of the van, whenever the guard moved, he did so in quick, jerky movements that caught me off guard and left an angry red ring on my wrist from the too-tight hold of the metal handcuffs. I could see him smirking from the corner of my eye.

I don't know what I thought I was in for when we got to court, but it certainly wasn't what I found. I think in my mind I was picturing some sort of sanity and order to counter the bizarre surrealism of the past twenty-four hours. I'd sit before authorities and be given a chance to explain the mistake, the giant misunderstanding that had landed me here. That's not what happened.

While we waited for my case to be called up, they freed me from the guard and instead cuffed me to a rail next to the toilets. The smell was nearly unbearable, and I hoped, whatever the outcome, that this would be over quickly. I didn't want to touch anything. I could feel the hot breath of the person behind me on the back of my neck and had the overwhelming feeling of being trapped in a crowded subway, only I wouldn't be spilling out onto the platform at the next stop, grateful for room to breathe and gasping for air. The person behind me coughed, and I felt the spray of wet spittle on the bare skin of my neck. I winced and choked down a sob.

When they finally called me forward, I was grateful just to be taken off the bar and moved away from the coughing man with the hot breath. The guards pushed me through a crowd, men shouting at me in Arabic from all angles and shoving business cards in my face.

At first, I didn't realize what was going on, and I felt remarkably like livestock at auction. But when a man was waved up by my guard and explained he was a lawyer from the US Embassy and to not engage with the others, I realized these men were all attorneys trying to secure me as a client. They were shouting things I couldn't understand, pushing and pulling at each other to get closer to me.

I looked around at the others awaiting their hearings and realized with startling astonishment—they weren't going after everyone with such fervor. Plenty of sorry souls sat ignored on the bar. Some were even trying to grab the attention of a lawyer. *It's because I'm white*, I thought with a sudden, sickening stab of privilege. They didn't see me as someone they could help. They weren't here doing their jobs. All they saw when they looked at me was a paycheck.

The lawyer from the embassy was talking to me, and I was trying to listen. His was the only voice around me I could, in theory, understand, but the discord around me was melding into a single, deafening thrum. The room was a rush of colors coming at me from all directions. The heat was suffocating. A river of sweat streamed down my back. My clothes stuck uncomfortably to my skin. Every sensation was distracting me from the words the lawyer was trying to make clear.

"Do you understand?" he was saying, his face close to mine and his frustrated, taut voice trying to remain calm while somehow also breaking through the clamor of shouting and a million conversations happening all around us.

"Hanna!" At first, I thought I was mistaken. Who was calling my name? Then, again: "Hanna!" I looked through the crowd, trying to find the source, while the guard pushed at my back and the embassy lawyer tried to guide me ahead by my arm. Just as I spotted the man pushing through the crowd, he shouted again. "Hanna! Amir . . . Uzair!"

The noise and chaos cleared. *Yes, that's me!*

Right in that moment, I knew. It was the clarity I needed to pull me back to the present, to try to grab some sort of control in this impossible situation. Amir and Uzair knew where I was. They'd sent help. I wasn't invisible or forgotten.

I ignored the embassy lawyer's insistence that I talk to no one, pushing my way toward the man. *Amir. Uzair.* I held on to the sound of their names in my ears as if I'd found them in that crowd.

"That's me!" I shouted as I closed the gap between myself and the man calling my name. "I'm Hanna!"

As soon as we reached each other, he wasted no time in his explanation, suspiciously eyeing the embassy lawyer over my shoulder as he spoke quickly. My friends had hired a lawyer, and he was on his way. This man had been sent ahead to make sure I knew to wait before accepting counsel from anyone else. As the embassy lawyer pleaded with me to step aside, to ignore this man, he fervently began listing names—Amir. Uzair. Mia. Taylor.

"Taylor?" I shouted and grabbed the man's forearm with my one uncuffed hand. "Did you say Taylor?"

The attorney looked bewildered. "Yes, Taylor, Amir, Uz—"

I spun toward the embassy lawyer. "My sister sent this man. My friends and my sister. This man stays."

I was told to admit to nothing. *Don't say anything.*

The day was long and miserable. I stood in the stench of the court and bit my lip as they counted my pills (melatonin, vitamins, supplements) and referred to a large bag of powder I knew very well was protein pancake mix.

I held my tongue with a knot in my gut as they weighed, in front of dozens of strangers, a minuscule amount of what was presumably cocaine—cocaine that could have come from anywhere—in a bag several times its weight. *Where had that come from?* I wondered as I watched helplessly. They counted the weight of the bag toward the total.

Then, they stuck me in a cell alone for hours. No food. No water. Eventually, the lawyers brought me a snack and something to drink. Though I still hadn't eaten since this nightmare had begun, I had little appetite.

In my mind, I kept seeing that bag of white powder, plastic wrapped several times over, and the smug look on the officials' faces as they read out the weight: five grams. I knew in the pit of my stomach that this misrepresentation—this downright intentional lie I had no power to speak against—was going to play a major role in whatever happened next.

I had been told not to speak, so what should I have said? Should I have shouted out in the middle of court, "Um, excuse me. That isn't my cocaine, but even if it was, why would you weigh it like *that*?!"

The weight of the situation was truly beginning to set in. I felt drastically out of my depth. Where was my lawyer? *Who* was my lawyer? I needed someone who could see just how wrong this all was.

Once again, I felt the sting of regret that I hadn't contacted my parents. *My parents. They'd know what to do. They'd know who to trust.*

Leaning against the cool metal bars of the otherwise stifling holding cell, I closed my eyes and released a silent prayer from somewhere deep within my soul.

TRACY

If emptiness has a smell, that's how I'd describe the house when we arrived home that morning. It was undoubtedly our house but lacking something essential, some key quality that pulled all the pieces together and really made it *home*.

Our drive had been filled with conversation and the beginnings of a game plan—*Who do we know that we can reach out to? Should we purchase tickets to fly to Aghasour immediately? Will we even be able to? Could they make exceptions to the COVID restrictions to let us through?*

We didn't know any more than we knew the night before after our call with Taylor. First step was to get home and start making calls.

We closed the door and shut out the winter cold. As I took off my coat and scarf, Kaya greeted me, weaving her way between my feet and rubbing against my boots. My heart sank a little as I looked down. I scooped her up and hugged her close.

That's when I caught just the faintest whiff. There it was. Fading in the house around us in the weeks since she'd left, but a trace lingered. A sweet, tangy, welcoming perfume. Unmistakably Hanna. Closing my eyes and breathing it in, I imagined opening my eyes again to find Hanna standing before me, safely at home. I knew it wasn't possible, but I clung to the thought.

I took another deep breath in as I scratched behind the cat's ears. Everything would be fine. We just needed somewhere to begin.

Jon began making coffee, and I retrieved my laptop from my weekend bag, bringing it to the dining room table. I grabbed a notebook and pen and sat down. We realized the first real step would likely come in the form of another call from Taylor or maybe Amir. But when your daughter is in an impossible situation on the other side of the world, waiting for anything at all hardly seems like an option. I began to make a list.

Flights to Aghasour, I jotted down, then finished it with a question mark. It *was* a big question mark, after all. Then, I continued my list, writing down anything that seemed pertinent or worth looking into.

US Embassy.

Dutch Embassy.

What police station?

Lawyer?

Senator's office.

Work in any branch of government, and you'll learn quickly that things move a lot faster when you know the right people. What could a senator from Idaho do for a girl behind bars thousands of miles away in Egypt? I honestly didn't know, but I would find out.

I began searching for flights. There were few, and they were incredibly expensive. COVID restrictions were definitely going to be an issue.

I continued to write notes. I fought the urge to Google "jail conditions Aghasour Egypt." Part of me needed to know; part of me knew that knowing wouldn't change anything except maybe my spirit.

Across the table, Jon was staring at his phone screen, his cup of coffee going cold in his hand. His face was set in a rigid gaze, and I imagined the worst—photos on his screen of squalid, inhumane conditions, horror stories of families fighting for years to free their loved ones.

I opened my mouth to say something—*let's try not to jump to conclusions*—but before I could get the words out, a strange ringing shattered the silence and derailed my train of thought. We both jumped.

At first, I assumed it was coming from Jon's phone. Then, our eyes met, and I could see he was just as confused as I was. Our eyes darted around the room, trying to place the jarring sound.

"Tracy," Jon said suddenly. "Your iPad!"

Sure enough, my iPad sticking out from under a stack of papers before us on the table was lit, a notification blinking in time with the unfamiliar ringtone. Moving before my brain could process anything, Jon shoved the papers aside, then seized the iPad and lifted it, revealing the call was coming through Facebook Messenger. It was an account we didn't recognize.

Without hesitating, Jon accepted the call.

"Hello?" The eagerness and desperation in my husband's voice was heart wrenching. Since our conversation with Taylor the night before, Jon hadn't cracked. Hadn't panicked. He remained steady as always. But slowly, I could see the weight building.

In the vacuous seconds before a reply, I realized I was hoping to hear Hanna's voice. Logic wasn't chiming in to offer any reason she'd be calling from some strange account, but in my heart, I desperately wanted it to be her. *Crisis averted. Major misunderstanding. I'm out now. No need to worry.*

At last, a man's voice came through. It was heavily accented and difficult to understand through the garbled connection.

"Hello . . . this is . . . Ahm . . ." The words were unclear, and I looked questioningly at Jon as if he might be able to make better sense of this. I grabbed the iPad urgently from him, stood, and lifted it in the air, willing the connection to improve.

Jon placed a hand on my elbow, gesturing for me to sit. The screen showed I had full service. This bad connection was not on our end.

"Hello," Jon answered back. Calm. Steady. "We cannot hear you very well. What is your name?"

Again, the response was muddled. Jon shook his head—*no use.* Time to move on. We had more important things to cover.

"Are you calling about our daughter?"

What else could it be? I held my breath, waiting for a reply.

"Yes, yes. Hanna."

My eyes locked with Jon's for a brief moment, and I sat forward in my chair. We didn't have this man's name, but he had Hanna's. It felt like a line cast out into the void, but it had caught something on the other end. If this man knew where Hanna was, there was no way we were letting go.

HANNA

I sat in that holding cell for what seemed like hours. It was beginning to have the feel of a nightmarish case of déjà vu. But eventually, they called me out again. And that was when I met Ahmed. The embassy lawyer played his hand again, giving me one last chance to not seek additional representation. But Ahmed was persistent. If this man had any connection to my friends, to my family, I needed to hear him out.

In truth, I didn't know who to believe. Even the embassy lawyer, someone who was supposed to be there representing me as a US citizen, seemed to be desperate for my business. Everyone was talking over each other, and my mind was reeling from exhaustion and trying to get my bearings on this situation. Suddenly, Ahmed shoved his phone toward me. There on the screen was a message from Amir.

Someone was talking to me—the embassy lawyer. "You need to focus. They are calling you up now." He prodded my arm, trying to pull me away, but my eyes were set on Amir's name on the phone screen. I lifted my gaze to meet the man's.

"My name is Ahmed. Your friends sent me." His eyes pleaded with me to believe him. "I will take care of you."

I had all of two seconds to consider.

"This man is my lawyer." The words were out of my mouth before I knew what was happening. But I knew it wasn't a mistake. Something was pulling me firmly in Ahmed's direction. It was time for a decision, and I had made it. We went through to hear the verdict of that first day, the initial charge we'd have the opportunity to plead down in the coming days.

As we walked toward the bench, Ahmed leaned in and spoke low. "This first charge will be worst-case scenario. You will not be able to argue it now. I've looked at your case. They made many mistakes. I will get you out of here."

A guard barked something at him then, and he averted his gaze. I realized later not even my lawyers were meant to be coaching me at this point. I had so many questions. I wanted to ask for time to talk with Ahmed. I wanted to tell him what I'd seen earlier when they'd weighed the cocaine.

But a guard shoved me in the back, and the judge—to the best of my ability to detect any official of stature in this joke of a court—began to speak. I couldn't understand a word he was saying. A man in a uniform to my right began to translate.

A few dizzying moments later, as they rushed me out of court, Ahmed trailed behind me, trying to reassure me before the guards shoved me back into the van.

"Remember," he urged. "This is just the first charge. We will get it down at the next court date."

I was pushed into the back of the van and onto the metal bench. On impact, I thought I might throw up. *I can't go back. What is happening? What is happening?*

I couldn't get the words out. Before me, Ahmed's face was disappearing as the van doors closed. The clink of metal on metal as they slapped my handcuff onto a bar welded to the van wall rang in my ears, and I could just barely make out Ahmed's urgent final words.

"Thirty days maybe. Maybe forty-five. Forget what they said. Thirty days. I will get you out."

And then, he was gone.

That gut feeling I'd had all day had been right. They were trying to pin me with drug trafficking. Intent to distribute. All the way back to the station, I held on to those words. *Worst-case scenario. I will get you out of here. I will take care of you. Thirty days maybe.*

"Fifteen years," the translator had said. Worst-case scenario was fifteen years.

TUESDAY, FEBRUARY 23RD

JON

It had been a full day since we'd spoken to Ahmed, the lawyer our daughter's friends had hired. I had texted Amir after our call to find out more about him. We hadn't been able to determine his name through the static of the call.

Amir told us the lawyer was called Ahmed Khaled. I Googled his name, but not much came up. Basically, we still knew nothing about him. He didn't seem to be part of a larger law firm. Tracy found his profile on Facebook, but still, we had few answers.

During that short and choppy call via Facebook Messenger, he had informed us he was on his way to meet with Hanna at court. Between the crackling of the connection, we were only able to isolate clips of information. He felt the authorities at the airport had made many mistakes in Hanna's arrest and processing. He said he was confident he could get her released. We should not deal directly with the embassy. We should trust him.

If I'm being honest, I really didn't know what to think. The connection was bad, so we only caught bits and pieces. We weren't even sure this was the person Hanna's friends had hired. It was an obscure call from an unknown number on a social media app. You hear the horror stories all the time, but when you find yourself in one, it's hard to know who to trust.

The problem was we had to find someone who could get us in touch with Hanna. We had to find out that she was okay, that she was safe. Could we trust this guy? Did Hanna's friends really find the best? Why did he not want the embassy involved? Every hour that passed was another hour we were in the dark.

We have no proof of Hanna's location, her well-being, or whether she is even . . .

The air that filled our home, the silence that filled the gaps in conversation—everything hung heavy with a feeling of helplessness.

I'm a scientist and researcher by training. How I approach almost all of life's bumps in the road could be described as purely pragmatic. That first day and night were no different—we didn't sit still and wait for the phone to ring. The only direction we felt any confidence in was forward. And so, Taylor kept trying the Dutch Embassy. Tracy reached out to our senator's office. They told us they couldn't do much until we got a privacy release statement from Hanna.

How are we going to get that? She is in some Godforsaken jail somewhere, and we have to get a privacy release first before they are going to do anything?

Tracy had begun gathering any information she could on the supplements in Hanna's luggage that had been mistaken for drugs. And I—well, I kept racking my brain, trying to find any path that would lead us to Hanna. We couldn't be there physically, so we needed to make a connection with someone who could.

That morning, it felt like treading water, flailing around, and grasping at lifelines that might not be there.

I sent a message to Amir.

Just confirming this is the same number you have for Ahmed, the lawyer?

I sent the number the man had given us the day before.

Though I was hoping for a simple confirmation, I could see that Amir was typing a response for longer than I expected. When his message finally came through, the weight on my shoulders that had been steadily mounting got much heavier.

Hey, Jon—yes, that's it. But would you mind holding off on contacting him this morning? There are some things you should be aware of before you speak to him again, and I'd like to share my personal thoughts on what we're dealing with. Do you have time for a call in an hour or so?

I let out a long, heavy breath that left my chest feeling hollow as I typed out a reply.

Of course. We are here. Please call when you can. Many thanks, Amir.

We were effectively placed on hold for the next hour and a half while we waited to hear from Amir. At many points, I felt the urge to call Ahmed anyway. Both Tracy and I were desperate to know that he'd met with Hanna as he'd said he would, were aching to hear that she was okay. Tracy kept working away diligently at her laptop, updating me on anything she'd found out. I kept busy, but focusing was hard.

When Amir finally called, I answered immediately. Even though we hadn't talked with Amir for almost a year and a half—well before the breakup—I'd always really liked the guy, and we got along well. We exchanged greetings that weren't forced exactly, but when you're in this type of situation, everyone knows there's no real time for pleasantries.

"So, what's going on, Amir?" I wanted to get down to it.

"I think maybe we've made a mistake. I'm not so sure about this lawyer." His directness was deflating.

"Okay," I responded after a pause. "What are your concerns?"

Amir went on to describe his interactions with Ahmed so far, emphasizing that the lawyer's main priorities seemed to revolve around payment. Amir, Taylor, and the others had already paid a significant sum of money to secure his services, but now he was requesting all the money now—upfront—before he would do anything further.

"I'm not saying he's a crook or has shady intentions," Amir continued. "But this is a difficult situation, and we all just want to help Hanna. We need to be sure he can be trusted to take this seriously—that he has the integrity we need to fight this."

The thought struck me suddenly that he could take the money today and tomorrow ask for more. *He could bleed us dry.*

How could we be sure? And what other options did we have at this time? Here we were, a band of Hanna's biggest champions—the people who would move mountains for her—scattered across the globe while trying to solve the same puzzle. Something was missing. Something was leaving us untethered.

I could feel my daughter slowly slipping out of reach.

As Tracy and Amir kept the conversation going, I felt the pressure continuing to build. *HOW ARE WE TO MOVE FORWARD? HOW ARE WE GOING TO GET HANNA OUT OF THERE!*

Through my distraction, I heard my name. I brought myself back to the present and asked Amir to repeat what he'd just said.

Amir replied, "Jon, I think we need to consider another lawyer." I went silent.

All I could think about was how we could find out where Hanna actually was and whether she was okay. *Is she safe?* And now, the only possible lifeline we had might be one we couldn't trust? *What if she is being hurt?* We were losing time.

These thoughts were swirling through my head and weighing me down. I shook myself out of my daze and concluded the call after telling Amir that I would reach out to a business contact I had in Egypt. In the meantime, I told Amir to stay connected with Ahmed. He was our only lifeline to Hanna. We needed to make sure she was safe. That was priority number one.

I needed fresh air. As I walked by the kitchen where Tracy was huddled over her computer again, she looked up at me with a worried expression. I continued past the living room, through the garage, and opened the door to the backyard. My thoughts were heavy and even more so with Amir's concerns ringing in my ears. *WHO COULD WE TRUST?*

HANNA

From Hanna's Journal
All there is to pass the time is sleep. And so, I sleep . . .
In the light of day, with my mind freed from my initial state of
shock, this place is somehow worse than I'd been letting myself believe
for the past two days. A single lightbulb is our only source of light. A
hole in the floor constitutes a toilet. No privacy.
No humanity.
The smell is insufferable. Cigarette smoke. Sweat. Burning plastic
(it seems these women will burn anything to heat their food). There
are smells I'd rather not try to identify, though it doesn't take much
imagination to figure them out.
Perhaps the cruelest part of the torture is the inability to discern the
time of day. Little light filters in through the window. I don't have the
courage—or words—to ask if anyone has a watch. I never knew it could
bother me this much, dig under my skin this deep, just to be unaware of
the hour. One moment, I'm fine; the next, I NEED TO KNOW.
Only prayers mark the passage of time.

———

The shock of returning to the cell put me into some sort of grief-in-
duced coma. When they dumped me back in, the door slamming
behind me once again, I pushed my way through the crowd in an
exhausted daze. Curious eyes followed me, but before I could talk

myself out of it, I walked straight to the hole I'd earlier hoped to never resort to using and finally relieved myself. The other women at least had the decency to look away as I cried, washing my hands in the stainless-steel basin that creaked as the water sputtered out.

I slept for the remainder of the day and into the following. Someone tried to rouse me once or twice, but I would only shake her off, roll over, and go back to sleep. The court proceedings—though that assumes some sort of order when there had been anything but—replayed in my mind, and my dreams were filled with the translator's words echoing over and over. *Fifteen years.*

When the spell of sleep threatened to wear off, my senses started to come back to life, though I tried hard to keep them at bay. It was difficult not to take in the smell—in the heat of the day, it seemed the air and the stench were one, indistinguishable from each other—but I did my best to avoid the appraising stare of a dozen watchful eyes as I looked around the cell.

Out of habit, I kept reaching into my pocket for the phone that wasn't there. Each time I came up empty, something within my chest wound tighter. It felt unnatural and increasingly frustrating, this disconnection from the outside world, but not only that, the sudden inability to do something as simple and mundane as telling the time. The window—no bigger than a concrete block—provided little clue. It was either night or day; anything more specific than that would have to be a guess.

The stress of it was enough to send me searching for sleep again, but no sooner had my mind finally succumbed when someone was shaking me awake. Forcefully. There was no ignoring it this time.

Before me was that same woman from the first night, seemingly unwilling to just give up on me and let me rot into a pile of clothes and nothing on the hard cell floor. As I relented and sat up, her expression took on that same frustrated satisfaction my mom would have when coming to wake me for school for the second or third time. For a moment, I had the urge to bark back at her like a cranky teenager. *What else am I supposed to do here?!*

She waited. We stared each other down.

I gave first, shrugging my shoulders in defeat and breaking eye contact. "Fifteen years." I spoke the words that had kept me gagged for the better part of the last day.

"What?" she asked incredulously, and I picked up on a tinge of what I mistook for amusement.

"Fifteen years!" I spat the words back at her. "That's what the translator said I could get!"

Her face relaxed into understanding, but she shook her head. "Always worst case first. No fifteen years." She waved the idea away with a dismissive hand. Then, she sat for a moment, taking me in. I imagined how horrid I must look and was suddenly very self-conscious.

She put a hand to her chest. "I'm Inara," she said.

Inara. So, the angel had a name.

"Hanna," I replied.

Behind her, one of the other women approached and knelt between us. She handed Inara two paper cups and something wrapped in paper. Inara responded in Arabic—something even I could recognize was a word of gratitude—and the woman nodded and walked away, but not before giving me a sympathetic half smile.

"Here," she said and pushed one cup toward me. She unwrapped the paper to reveal two pieces of a pita-like bread. "We save this for you. While you sleep. It is not good to miss meals."

I took the bread and bit into it. It was stale, but it was calories, and my stomach was finally demanding I put something into it.

"What your lawyer say?" Inara asked, pointedly turning the conversation back to the subject of my court appearance.

Again, I shrugged, chewing. "Thirty days. Maybe forty-five."

Her espresso-brown eyebrows raised, and she nodded in agreement. "See, no fifteen years. Thirty days, you can do." When my eyes shot down to the floor, she leaned down with me to retrieve my gaze. "I've done nineteen already."

I had no response. I strongly suspected this woman I'd known for barely two days was made of a lot tougher stuff than I was. But still, what could I do? Balk at the idea of thirty days? She'd been here nineteen days. Should I cry and tell her I could hardly stomach nineteen more *seconds*?

I bobbed my head in reluctant agreement, then downed my cup of water in two gulps. I tried not to think of the creaking, sputtering sink with the rusty mineral stains that ran behind it down the back wall. We sat in silence for some time.

"I don't know if I can do this." The words suddenly poured from my mouth, and my throat tightened as the tears welled in my eyes. "I don't know how you do it, but I . . . I don't know if I can go another day—another minute—not knowing what's going on out there. Not even knowing what time of—"

Abruptly, a disembodied, melodic noise rang out somewhere beyond the cell walls, stealing the words straight from my mouth. There was an instant, collective movement of shuffling as the women in the cell clambered to their feet. I saw then that some had prayer rugs, and I watched as they placed them carefully on the floor, smoothing and straightening them with care.

As Inara moved to position herself accordingly, she met my eyes and whispered, "Dhuhr. Afternoon prayer."

Of course. Prayer.

I swallowed my tears and sat silently, respectfully, while the women around me prayed. For the second time since I'd arrived, I felt a wave of calm flood my body, much like the sudden flush of embarrassment but more soothing, more grounding. The call to prayer being delivered through a speaker system somewhere outside the jail walls was achingly familiar. Though I did not know the words or the language in which they were spoken, I closed my eyes and was taken back in time.

I was in Cairo with my now ex-boyfriend, Amir. We were strolling through the picturesque Al-Azhar Park, an oasis of green in the middle of the bustling city, when the call to prayer began. I watched in reverent silence as the world around us went still, and nearly all turned their thoughts and attention and, indeed, their physical bodies to God.

Since I was dating an Egyptian man, I knew, of course, of the daily prayer, but this was the first I'd witnessed it on a large scale. I was raised Christian—not Muslim—but I've always been a deeply spiritual person, which I believe transcends the labels of denomination.

In that moment, I felt a sudden and profound connection with my surroundings—the greenery of the park, the unifying murmur of the people, the hum of the city. The first tendrils of roots were sprouting. I knew then I'd find my way back to Egypt.

"Dhuhr," he'd whispered, meeting my eyes. "Afternoon prayer."

Amir had explained to me later that the time for Dhuhr, same as the other four prayers throughout the day, was determined based on the position of the sun and could be different from one day to the next. I'd always considered myself a true child of the moon, but still, the beauty in this spoke to me.

"That seems hard to plan around something that occurs five times a day," I'd jested.

Amir shrugged as we walked. "Well, generally speaking, Dhuhr is usually sometime around one."

"Sometime around one," I repeated and laughed. "I'll put it in my calendar."

Back in the cell, a solitary tear escaped my tightly closed eyes and carved a path down my cheek. There it was, simple and plain as day. An answer to a prayer I had not known I was praying.

It was sometime around one.

TRACY

The sound of Jon's office chair sliding backward and his footsteps as he approached the kitchen where I was sitting quickly got my attention. I was concerned with how he was processing this all. The phone call with Amir was just one more worry.

Jon has always been the one that people lean on for problem-solving. He is so good at breaking down an issue and building a plan forward. But we had never been through anything like this. This was deeply personal. One of his greatest fears as a parent was unfolding before his very eyes.

My gaze followed him as he walked past and then traveled down the hall. The weight on his shoulders was clearly visible. When I opened my mouth to ask if everything was okay, he waved a hand toward me, wordlessly urging me to continue my work. I tried to gather my focus.

I went back to my research, but my thoughts had walked right out the door with Jon as he briskly exited into the garage.

He'll be okay.

I sent up a silent prayer.

JON

As the door opened, I heard the familiar sounds of our backyard sanctuary—the birds, the wind softly blowing through the trees, our wind chime . . . And then, suddenly, it all vanished. I looked up and was startled by the silence. Complete silence. Not a sound. A wave of calm came over me. It showered my body with a complete feeling of serenity.

That familiar blanket of peace immediately transported me to years earlier in Turkey. I was stepping inside a modest little house on Mount Koressos, just outside Ephesus. It was called the House of the Virgin Mary where it was believed she had lived her last years. It was serene; it was silent. I'd experienced a feeling of complete peace where all tensions completely melted away.

My thoughts brought me back to the present. I was standing in our backyard, but I could have been in that chapel. I was at peace. My head was clear. In my mind, I heard—felt—the words pulsating through me.

Give it to me.

Give it to me, Jon.

I heard it again. *Give it to me. Trust me. Give it to me. I am here.*

The stress in my body washed away, and my mind was cleared of worries. I had this sense of euphoria. I could think clearly again—crystal clear. I felt calm, assured. The weight I had been carrying on my shoulders totally disappeared.

I put complete trust and confidence in that reassuring voice. *The voice of God? The voice of God!* I know it sounds crazy. But it was real. It was real. I cannot deny it.

I believe in logic, in evidence that can be observed and recorded. But this was real. Very real. When reason and effort and my own strength had failed me, when the tension in my head had become a deafening roar, another voice—steady and sure—had cut through the noise and made itself heard.

I was overwhelmed. I wanted to cry, I wanted to laugh, I wanted to sing. Finally, I could see the path ahead of me—ahead of us. I could see the thread that would hold us all together. In the most uncertain moment of my life, I had clarity.

I filled my lungs with an invigorating rush of crisp, cool air and let out a silent, *Thank you.* Then, I turned and headed back to the house.

I left the backyard with a spring in my step, elated to share my experience with Tracy just as I had years ago in Turkey.

Trust me. Give it to me. I am here.

HANNA

From Hanna's Journal

There are many ways to learn a lesson. I guess this is mine. I'm beginning to wonder if that is why I'm here.

When I arrived, there were maybe twelve women in this cell, and even then, it felt like too many. Suddenly, there are nineteen of us. We're sleeping on top of each other when we have space to sleep at all. We rest in unspoken shifts, taking advantage of empty patches of concrete floor whenever a space large enough to lie down opens up.

Inara told me a story of a lady who was locked in here for five days with her baby. A baby. In this place. That would never happen in the US. At night, when they brought dinner, they brought formula and diapers, which seems easy to mistake for compassion if you can forget for a moment that this is no place for a baby to begin with. I asked what she'd done that was so bad they locked her up with her baby still in her arms.

"Begging," Inara said, looking at me blankly, ". . . for food to feed her baby."

Tell me, who in that situation committed the real crime?

Inara's words have been sinking in, and my eyes and ears are opening wide. What if I'm here to listen? To learn, to reflect, to be a witness for others? To hear what God might be trying to tell me?

During that afternoon prayer, I think I truly saw my surroundings for the first time. Ugly, yes. Suspicious stains on the floor where these women bowed their heads in prayer. Paint peeling from the concrete block walls. Flies clinging to the mesh grate over the single window as if they too were in need of fresh air.

It has to be bad when even the flies are desperate to escape.

But there was beauty here too. It was impossible not to see it in that moment through the sharp contrast of the conditions and all those women praying in unison. I'd been so wrapped up in my own experience—and I don't think anyone could blame me for that, really—that I hadn't truly considered the others. Why were they here? What had they done? I wondered then what prayers were on their hearts that afternoon.

Having some idea of the time brought me a sense of calm I hadn't experienced in days. When all control is stripped away, it is strange what little things will bring you comfort. I felt like I had taken something back, reclaimed some small piece of dignity. I sat and soaked in the relief for the rest of prayer.

When it ended, everyone returned to their favorite pastimes—smoking, sleeping, standing at the cell door and yelling at the guards. Inara returned to our spot and picked up her bread again.

"What you do anyway?" she asked after a moment.

"Oh . . ." I hesitated, not knowing where to begin. "They think I had drugs. At the airport."

Inara looked up quickly, and her eyes scanned the room as if to see who might be listening. She lowered her voice when she responded.

"Drugs is not good here. Some ways, drugs worse than killing." She raised a single finger to her lips in a hushing motion.

Got it.

"I didn't," I began very quietly. "But okay, I understand." After a moment, I worked up the courage to ask. "Why are you here?"

Inara looked again around the room, but this time, she spoke at a regular volume. "Why are any of us?" she said. "Some of us, bad things. Some, less bad. Some, nothing."

Inara's English was sparse but strong enough that we could piece together a conversation. As we nibbled at our bread, she recounted the various offenses—or lack thereof—of our other cellmates and some who had come before us. I couldn't be sure whether it was the bread or these stories that left a heavy weight in the pit of my stomach.

It seemed we were a mix of violent criminals, women who were simply trying to make ends meet, and those who were quite clearly just victims of a very broken system. Inara pointed out a woman— purple and yellowing bruises covering her cheeks, one eye swollen shut—whose husband had attacked her for giving directions to a male tourist on the street. Police responded and threw them both in jail. Her husband was down the hall. Then, Inara tilted her head to another woman, sitting alone in the corner, silent and still.

"Killed her own child," she said.

And then, there was me. A selfish, ignorant, and stupid American girl who could have just thought this through a moment longer, maybe listened to her parents' advice a little better. Then, maybe she'd have avoided this whole mess.

I wrapped up my portion of bread. I no longer had an appetite.

"When you go back to court?" Inara asked, likely picking up on the fact that the conversation had turned a bit too sour for me.

"Tomorrow," I replied. "Maybe they'll let me go?"

"Maybe," she said and gave that same warm half smile that felt like a consolatory pat on the back.

I'm not going anywhere, am I?

I pushed the thought away. It would return later when I put my head down to sleep. For now, I wanted to hold on to the little bit of sanity I'd managed to find.

"I leave, maybe a few days," Inara said, and that sanity threatened to abandon me right then and there. Instead, I let it sink in. I was beginning to feel like this process—coming to terms with my situation—was a bit like quicksand. I was slowly sinking, but I'd never fully settle.

After a moment passed, Inara spoke again.

"You cannot sleep all day. Sad. Look around." She gestured around the crowded cell. "We all sad. We all tired. But we still pray. What else we going to do?"

I didn't have an answer. *Sleep. Chain-smoke. Go mad.*

"This," she jabbed a finger at her piece of half-eaten bread. "This feeds body. Prayer feeds soul."

She reached across and grabbed my hand. She squeezed it in her own.

"Now, only God speak to you." She raised a hand to indicate the world outside the cell walls. "Listen."

JON

I returned to the house with a sense of relief. It felt like a ton of weight had just been lifted from my shoulders, and in its place, there was a comforting feeling of hopeful trust. Once the dense fog and doubt had cleared from my mind, I was able to approach the situation with surprising clarity and peace. I didn't have all the answers. Not even close. In fact, I knew nothing more than I had moments earlier. But what I did have was a renewed sense of direction.

For the moment, Ahmed remained our only real connection to Hanna, and we needed to hang on to that until we knew more. Patience was going to be key in our fight.

Tracy and I discussed our next moves, and then I texted Amir. *Let's stay with this lawyer for now.*

I went on to explain to him that we had a release form from our senator's office that we needed Hanna to sign if we had any hopes of getting the embassy involved. Since Ahmed would soon be traveling to see her in court, he was our best shot at making that happen.

It wasn't long before Amir messaged back. Apparently, Ahmed was expressing some hesitance in delivering the form. The idea of involving the embassy was making him uneasy, and he was pushing back at our requests.

"This guy is just after the money. He wants to milk this case!" I mumbled upon reading Amir's message. My mistrust of Ahmed was intensifying, but the clarity I'd found that morning was still there, like a refreshing stream of reassurance washing over me and keeping me focused. I messaged back.

Tell him this is absolutely critical to us, and we need that form signed.

I took a breath, then began typing out another message.

And then I want you to do me a favor, Amir. Please arrange a video call with him. We need to all look each other in the eye and get everything on the table. Let's hear him out and find out if we are all on the same page.

I trusted Amir would set up the call, and while questions of doubt and uncertainty still plagued my mind, I knew that until that conversation, I needed to stay open. Open to the possibility that this was the correct path, that we were heading in the right direction.

Moments later, my phone chimed. Tracy had set up a new WhatsApp group, and in it were the two of us, Amir, Taylor, and—somewhat to my surprise—Ahmed. She'd named it "Egypt Hanna Team." I looked up from my phone and caught her eye. She gave an encouraging nod.

"That's what we need to be to make this work," she said. "A team."

On our side of the world, Hanna's team did what we could in the moment. While we waited for news—any news—we continued working away at our lists and recorded a message for Hanna. We sent it to Amir and hoped it would make it to our daughter. We needed her to know we were the last thing she should be worrying about. *We've got this. We are fighting for you.* We needed her to know she had a team in her corner.

A short while later, the "team" received its first message.

I am on my way to Hanna.

Ahmed was going to see her. Hope swelled that he would give her our message, that he would follow through and get the form signed. We sent our sincere thanks.

You are welcome. No need to thank me. She is my sister now. Don't worry.

WEDNESDAY, FEBRUARY 24TH

HANNA

From Hanna's Journal
  *Part of me knew there was never any real hope of leaving this cell
for good when I walked out this morning. Still, returning this evening
felt like a gut punch.*
  The justice system here is a mess.

———

Ahmed and I met amidst the chaos of the court around us. Though
I'd seen little evidence of it during my trip to court before, I'd imagined some quiet room where Ahmed and I would be able to meet
and discuss my case in privacy. I guess I've seen too many courtroom dramas. Scratch that—I guess I've seen too many *American*
courtroom dramas.

  The reality of the situation was this: I was conversing with
my lawyer in the chaos of what seemed like a hundred different
conversations at once—made worse by the fact that it all, quite
literally, sounded foreign to me. I remained cuffed, once again,
to a bar outside the men's toilets, and the stench was borderline

unbearable. Worse, its occupants seemed to feel the need to walk *through* me rather than around while entering and exiting.

At first, I had a hard time focusing on anything Ahmed was saying. I looked around the hall at the other detainees awaiting their hearings, some having already heard their verdicts. I searched for signs on their faces that there had been good news. I was desperate for any reassurance that this wasn't the purgatory I had a nagging feeling it was. All I found were sullen faces, anger, and expressions that spoke of resignation.

"Hanna," Ahmed said, no nonsense in his voice. His tone from the moment we began made it clear there would be no time for small talk—not that I wanted to talk about the weather. He had an agenda and we had—were allowed—very little time to take care of necessary business. It was apparent that I was there for the court's purposes, not my own. I was beginning to wonder what rights I was entitled to in this country—in this system—if any at all.

"First . . ." he continued, taking his phone from his pocket. As though he'd magically produced a fountain before a man stranded in a desert, this had my attention. "I have a message from your parents."

I could feel my heart thrashing against my rib cage.

"Can I call them?" I blurted out, reaching for the phone.

He pulled it back, shaking his head. "No, I'm sorry. It is not permitted."

Deflating, I sank back against the wall, only to be shoulder-checked by yet another man coming out of the toilets, wiping wet hands on his pants.

"But they recorded a message for you," he quickly added, clearly tuned in to my disappointment.

He held the phone up between us and leaned in close. I saw him scan the hall and wondered if even this delivery of a simple message from my parents was crossing some line.

I could barely make out my parents' words over the disorder around us and a cacophony in my head I could only suspect was the sound of my own heart breaking. The overwhelming love and reassurance in their voices couldn't mask their pain. Pain put there by me. *I will spend a long time making up for this.*

I wanted to listen to their message over and over again, wanted to somehow carry it back to the cell and fall asleep to it playing in my ears at night. But I only got to hear it once. As soon as it finished playing, Ahmed stood up straight, and I could tell we were moving on.

"Now, I need you to record a message for them," he instructed.

"But I can't call?" I asked again, confused.

He shook his head.

Over the next several minutes, Ahmed coached me through the message I would send. The first several tries were aborted mid-recording.

"No, no, you cannot say that," Ahmed urged. "You'll only worry them. Please stick to what I've told you."

Stunned into submission, I repeated the rehearsed phrases back on autopilot, no longer recognizing the sound of my own voice by the time we were finished.

"Mom. Dad. I'm doing good. Thank you so much for your support, your love, and your help. Things are fine. They look like they're . . ." I stumbled briefly, and a look of concern flashed across Ahmed's face. ". . . looking up. I'm so sorry to put you guys through this. I love you a lot and hope to see you soon . . ." I swallowed what felt like a fistful of tears. "It's okay. Everything is okay. I love you." Ahmed hastily hit stop.

Finally satisfied, he nodded. "Good, good, okay . . ."

As he said this, a guard approached and forcefully grabbed my wrist. In an instant, I was off the bar on the wall, cuffed to the guard, being dragged off toward the courtroom.

Ahmed kept up, and my eyes searched his for answers. "It's okay. You're being called up." Then, he made a point to hold my gaze, his eyebrows raised as if to say, *This is important. Are you paying attention?*

His hand disappeared inside his coat, and as I was still moving along the crowded hallway, I suddenly felt something slip into my hand. A folded piece of paper and a ballpoint pen.

"Sign," Ahmed mouthed. "Now."

To say the next several moments were stressful would be the understatement of the century. Ahmed and I were separated in the courtroom. I was forced to sit on a bench, still handcuffed to the guard, while Ahmed waited on the sidelines. My supposed right to counsel felt like a joke. Was that even a thing here?

Everyone's cases were being heard in this very public forum, but I could understand none of it. The guard, seemingly paying attention to the case currently before the judge, was momentarily distracted. As discreetly as I could, having only one free hand, I unfolded the paper Ahmed had slipped to me. It was some sort of privacy release form. I didn't have time to read the details. The moment the pen touched the paper, the guard snatched both from me. He said nothing, but his eyes were full of reproach.

Tears welling, I looked up and knew instantly that Ahmed had seen. I could tell he was trying not to look disappointed and could see the wheels in his head turning. If the form was so important, why wasn't I allowed to just sign it?

I was surprised to find that when I was called up, they removed the cuffs and ushered me into a room before a judge. Ahmed and the translator stood in silence while the judge quickly rattled off a series of statements. No one translated for me. My mind was still on the message from my parents and the form now in the guard's pocket.

A few short moments later, as we left the room, I could sense the guards were eager to get me back to the station. They stood waiting with handcuffs, and my heart began to race in my chest. I wasn't ready to go back.

Ahmed pulled one of them aside, leaned in close, and spoke in hushed words I couldn't hear. Then, he disappeared for a moment down the hall. When he returned, he came straight up to me. Quickly and quietly he said, "You're going to the toilet. You will be alone only for a minute. Look behind the toilet. Sign it and leave it there."

I could only nod in response.

The door to the toilet closed shut behind me, and I quickly opted to hold my breath. I had mistakenly thought for a brief moment that I might also take this opportunity to use the restroom in private for once, but what I found myself faced with made me certain I wanted to touch as few surfaces as possible.

If the smell had been bad standing outside the room, I can't even begin to describe what it was like standing within it. The floor was wet and tacky, the soles of my shoes making a sickening sucking sound with every movement, and unidentifiable stains streaked both the toilet itself and every surface along its perimeter.

Okay. Let's get this over with.

Quickly, I approached the toilet and reached around the back of the bowl. My hand brushed the pipes, and what I hoped was only condensation clung to my bare skin. I shivered in revulsion. Then, my fingers found it. The form, folded up, a pen tucked inside.

I stood up straight and made quick work of unfolding it. As I did, there was a banging on the door. I was being told to hurry it up.

"Just a minute," I called in response.

I still had no time to read what the form was about. Oh well. I looked around, trying to decide what surface was suitable enough to write on. Finding none, I decided on my own thigh. Crouching awkwardly, I scribbled my signature where indicated as another pounding on the door echoed in the small, filthy room. I briskly folded the paper back up and tucked it into the waistband of my pants. I wouldn't risk having it confiscated again.

More banging accompanied by an indiscernible but urgent command. I looked at the sink, then down at the hand that had just blindly felt around the back of that toilet. It was worth risking another scolding.

Emerging a moment later, shaking the water from my hands, a guard glared down at me.

"I had to wash my hands," I offered, holding them up for him to see.

No sooner had I slipped the paper back to Ahmed than I was cuffed and rushed away to the van. On the ride back to the jail, my head hitting the metal wall behind me with every pothole and stone in the road, I felt the smallest bit of relief creep in. For what felt like the first time all day, I exhaled. Closing my eyes, I felt a rush of gratitude. *Thank you, God.* Finally, I had been able to do something to help myself, to help my family in their efforts to aid me. Even if I'd had to steal the moment in a men's toilet.

As soon as I returned to the cell, my eyes scoured the room. I needed something to write on. My search ended at the trash can beside the sink. Pushing aside remnants of spoiled food, I retrieved a paper grocery bag folded several times over.

"Yes!" I exclaimed aloud. Several women turned at my outburst.

It was a miracle the bag hadn't been used by one of the other women. I sat down and got to work. From the rolled-up waistband of my pants, I pulled out the ballpoint pen Ahmed had left with the paperwork behind the toilet. Carefully, I tore a small section from the bag. On it, I recorded a message. A message to my parents, full of all the words I hadn't been able to find, hadn't been allowed to say, in the one I'd recorded earlier.

When I finished writing, I placed the note in Inara's hands, tears in my eyes. Any moment, she'd be called to court, and this note was a second chance to share something true with my parents. Something that could bring them some comfort in the same way their message would replay through my mind all night. I closed her fingers around the crumpled paper and squeezed her hand tight.

"Please, please get this to my lawyer, Ahmed. It is for my parents. Please."

She nodded, and I knew then that, if nothing else, she would try. When Inara was finally called, I sat down, smoothed out a new section of the paper bag, and began to write. Not a letter this time but a record. Starting with that very moment everything had gone wrong at airport security, I began to journal everything I could remember since.

From Hanna's Journal

My next court date is in fourteen days. March 9. Ahmed seemed hopeful, confident even, that there's a chance I could be leaving here for good that day. Fourteen days.

For now, I will wait out these dark hours and put my energy and thoughts into staying strong until that day finally comes. I'll sleep when I have room to lie down. I'll spend time in conversation with God when language fails me. I'll focus on everything I have, and I'll find compassion for these women around me—even the one who stole my underwear. Many of these women have no idea when they'll leave or what they'll return home to when they do. For some, I suspect it will be the same situations that landed them here in the first place.

My privilege is never more apparent to me than when I look around this room at all those women, and I think about the moment those cell doors finally open for me . . . I'll run fast and far and never look back.

TRACY

It was as if everything in our life was suddenly separated into two distinct periods: before and after. Everything following that midnight text from Tracy was tinged with anxiety and grief. Sleep was brief and restless at best, and the mornings brought with them a hollowness, a dull ache that signaled to my waking body something was not quite right in the world. Then, the realization would settle in: *our daughter is locked up thousands of miles away—beyond our reach.*

Rest is necessary but cruel in that way. A few hours of peace—if you're lucky enough to actually fall asleep—but waking is like receiving the unfathomable news all over again. Each morning: wake, remember, process.

The first thing we did when we woke up was reach for our phones. That was another problem with sleep—while we were sleeping, Hanna was presumably awake, along with the rest of that side of the world. While we slept, things were happening—things were moving ahead without us.

But it seemed that more often than not, we'd wake to find no real news. Nothing had happened while we'd slept. Hanna was still sitting behind bars, and we were left with a handful of hours to get something—anything—accomplished before her side of the world went to sleep and we were left to wait for another day.

As a result, there were many nights I never truly got to sleep. Instead, I'd diligently chip away at anything I could throughout the night or check my phone frequently for news, desperate to know what was happening.

In the early hours of Wednesday morning, my phone lit up in the dark. It was a message from Ahmed.

The day before had been full of turmoil. We'd had an anxious conversation with Amir. Together, we'd examined our doubts from every angle, stuck in a holding pattern of not knowing if the lawyer could be trusted, whether we'd made the right decision to work with him.

When Jon abruptly left the house for the backyard, I was deeply concerned that the question of trust would be a truly impossible one to answer. He disappeared into the backyard a broken man. He returned a fortified one. It was a truly incredible transformation, and the peace he brought with him back into our home shed a new light on our situation.

Working together that morning—communicating decisive next steps with Amir, recording our message to our daughter to remain strong and know we were here for her—it was clear to me that we needed to remain unified. Working in our own individual silos would not help us rise to these challenges that, at the time, seemed so impossibly large.

And yet Ahmed, the person with the best chances at reaching Hanna, still felt like an outsider. We'd gone to bed at the end of the day knowing he had the form from our senator's office and had our recorded message, but we also had reservations that were making us continue to question his intentions.

I knew that Jon was anxiously awaiting a face-to-face call with the lawyer—that he wanted to level with him and bring some transparency to this tangled web. For me, as the hours passed and sleep eluded me, the tasks we'd given Ahmed felt like tests. How would that call play out if he couldn't pass them? What would it mean if he didn't follow through?

At 3:00 a.m., I received a message from Ahmed. It was a picture of the form, and there at the bottom was Hanna's signature! It was unmistakably hers. Just seeing her handwriting—it looked good, strong—felt like a beautiful message from Hanna. It lifted my heart. *She is alive. Thank God!*

In another message, Ahmed filled us in on how they'd pulled it off—and how they almost hadn't. I was beginning to get an idea of how the justice system in Egypt was stacked against us. Cooperation from anyone on the other side was looking slim, so cooperation with each other was essential.

When Ahmed delivered that form, it felt like a sign. A sign that we were heading in the right direction with the right people.

The form wasn't the only thing Ahmed delivered that morning. When the recording came through, I shook Jon awake beside me.

"Jon!" I urgently roused him. "Jon, Ahmed has sent a message from Hanna!"

He was upright in an instant.

We sat huddled over my phone, and my hand shook as I pressed play.

"Mom. Dad . . ." The sound of my daughter's voice instantly flooded my heart, and tears began to stream from my eyes.

We listened to her message several times. It was easy to tell she was not herself. Her voice was tense; the message felt forced. But we finally had what we had been anxiously waiting for—our daughter was alive. The message, while heartbreaking, was the greatest gift.

While we savored the message, Ahmed filled us in on the other details of the day. At Hanna's hearing, the judge had ordered an initial period of fifteen days for Hanna, pending lab results from the evidence collected. Fifteen days. That would be March 10. It seemed like a lifetime away.

Ahmed also explained a bit of his initial hesitancy involving the form. First, he had known it would be difficult. The police commissioner was already giving him a lot of hassle, and he sensed we had a tough road ahead with him. We needed to tread lightly. Which brought him to the second reason for his reluctance to involve the embassy—Ahmed wanted to make sure everything moved through him. He wanted the senator's office and the embassy to stay focused on getting the lab results that were so important for Hanna's next hearing. That was where they ought to apply their pressure. He worried any perceived pressure from all these different angles placed on that police commissioner could have dire consequences.

According to Ahmed, the place they had her was not good. But there were worse places. He made it clear that what we absolutely did not want was for that police commissioner—a man we were beginning to get a not-so-pretty picture of—to get antsy and say, "Get her out of here!" That, he imparted, could be very bad.

We absorbed everything Ahmed told us through his series of messages and looked at each other. Some of this made sense, but were they just excuses? We couldn't know for sure.

And then, there we were, sitting wide awake in bed just after three in the morning with what seemed would be the majority of news and progress for the day. The hearing was over; Hanna was already back in jail.

"You should try to sleep," Jon suggested as he turned away from my bedside light. I suspected he knew that would be a losing battle for me.

As I lay awake, my mind ran through every scenario forward and back. I recalled the items on my to-do lists and mentally rearranged them based on order of importance. As the minutes turned into hours, I went over every word of Hanna's nearly robotic message, analyzing every syllable and wondering how long it would be before I would speak to her again. I longed to hear her voice. Her *real* voice. I ached to feel connected to my daughter.

As the sun rose that morning, I was already at it, pouring a second cup of coffee, when my phone buzzed. It was a message from my sister, the only loved one I had confided in about our situation so far.

Woke up in the middle of the night praying. I'm here for you.

Smiling, I set down my mug to type out a reply, but before I could hit send, my phone buzzed again. This time, the message was from Ahmed. In it, a photo of what appeared to be a torn section of brown shopping bag . . .

Mom and Dad,

Hearing your voices today broke my heart. I am so sorry for everything. I can't describe how bad I feel for putting you through this. Please don't worry about me. God will take care of me. I can feel Him. He tells me that you are doing everything to help me.

I had to read over the first lines more than once. The handwriting was difficult to decipher in parts, frantically scribbled and slanting across the surface. But it was familiar. With the first several lines clear, I read on.

There is an angel in here. Her name is Inara. All I could do was sleep, but she stayed by my side to make sure I was all right. She speaks some English. I'm giving her this note. I now understand the power of prayer.

I love you. I will be okay.

Hanna

As I finished reading, relief flooded my whole body, and I clutched my phone to my chest, tightly closing my eyes. There it was. That connection I'd been missing for days. There *she* was. My daughter. My Hanna.

As I read her note, her voice rang loud and true in my mind, and the words she'd written spoke to my heart. It was incredible. I hadn't heard her speak about God for years, not since she was a child.

The gratitude I felt in that moment was overwhelming.

The tie I felt to Hanna, the exhilaration I felt at simply knowing she was alive, renewed something within me. Feeling uplifted and energized, I went to the kitchen table and opened my laptop. I navigated to Facebook and typed out a new status.

What do you do when your heart is breaking? You call on your prayer warriors. The ones who won't ask questions but will offer prayer for God's strength and God's speed for resolution. God's intervention is so needed. I believe in the power of prayer. I would appreciate yours!

With the click of a button, that little bit of our story was out there in the world. I wasn't ready to share details, but that didn't mean we had to walk this journey alone. And I knew we wouldn't.

I leaned back in my chair, my coffee mug snug in my hands. I didn't have to wait long. One like. Then another. One comment—"Covering you in prayer, Tracy." Then another. As the goodwill and generosity rolled in, my heart filled with a warmth that began to radiate outward, spreading through my whole body. I sat alone in my kitchen, but I was not alone. Hanna was not alone either.

THURSDAY, FEBRUARY 25TH

HANNA

From Hanna's Journal
  Tired, tired, and more tiredness.
  It's crazy how up and down I am in this place. One moment, I'm feeling optimistic, settled with my situation. I've finally stopped sinking in the quicksand, and now it is only a matter of waiting. But then, the next minute (like now), I'm in my head and depressed like I'll go crazy if I sit still for one more minute.
  It's been six days, and I still haven't brushed my teeth.
  My spirit is close to breaking.

Under any other circumstances, you'd think someone given nothing to do but think and sleep would be, if nothing else, well-rested. That was not the case.

Thinking proved to be treacherous at times. If I couldn't get myself in the right headspace to a place where I could reflect peacefully, meditate, or mentally plan all the ways I would better myself once I was out, my thoughts tended to veer into dangerous territory. The more I slept, it seemed, the more exhausted and groggier my mind and body became. Short of a miracle, I was looking at thirteen more days in this place. I needed something else to pass the hours.

I spent some time organizing my stuff, and there wasn't much of that to keep track of. I wasn't allowed to keep many of my belongings in the cell, but Ahmed managed to get me a clean blanket and pillow, which, honestly, made a world of difference when I did sleep.

One thing I was allowed to keep was my money. That seemed odd to me at first until I realized that I would *need* that money to survive in here. Very little was supplied to us. Meager meals and that sugary "juice." We dared not drink the water from the same sink we washed our hands and filthy clothes in. If we wanted water or anything else, it had to be purchased. Still, there were limits to what money could buy.

There were times I thought I'd give up every dime I had left in exchange for a book. My body could survive, even if just barely, on the food provided. My mind was starving.

The moment I got my hands on that paper bag, I filled my time as much as I could with writing, recording everything I could remember about those first few days. I transcribed everything from the mundane—wondering how many calories were in the unleavened bread and over processed feta cheese that constituted many of our meals—to the horrific. And there was plenty of each to go around.

In the early, dark hours of that Thursday morning, painful wails and cries for help erupted from the men's block down the hall. The sound of fists on the metal cell door and boots kicking at the concrete block walls—a dreadful mixture of anguish and outrage.

"What's going on?" I asked Inara as I forced myself upright. The look on her face was somber.

"Hours, they asked for help," she said. "No one came."

Looking around, I saw many of the women wore the same tired, helpless stares.

"Help for what?" I turned back to Inara.

"A man was sick," she replied. Then, the shouting down the hall reached a fever pitch as the authoritative voices of the guards joined in. The sound of the cell door swinging open reached my ears. The commotion began to fizzle out, leaving only a few isolated protests from men who were beyond backing down, miles past caring when to keep their mouths shut.

I couldn't make out anything those men were saying, but Inara's deeply troubled face told me she had a good idea of what was going on.

The cell door closed again, and as I opened my mouth to say something—*maybe they'd finally come to help?*—I registered another sound layered under the steps from the guards' boots echoing down the hall. A sickening sound, quiet yet unmistakable. Cloth on concrete, something heavy being pulled—dragged—unceremoniously down the corridor. As it moved past our cell, I felt the whole room hold its breath.

We sat still in the aftermath for what seemed like hours but was probably only minutes.

What just happened?! Where the hell am I?!

It felt unreal. I could hardly believe my eyes when, one by one, the women in my cell slid back into their routines. Back to sleep. Back to smoking. Like it had never happened at all.

How is this real?

And an hour later, all I could think about was where the hell was my toothbrush.

JON

Thursday, Amir had organized a time for a call with Ahmed. It would be mid-afternoon our time, late evening for them. The day passed achingly slowly as we waited.

When the time came for the call, at first, it didn't work. We'd arranged the call on Zoom, but the connection just wouldn't stick. We ended up going back to a video call via Facebook Messenger.

The technical difficulties weren't easing our anxiety. We needed the video call to work. We needed the opportunity to *see* Ahmed—face to face. It was vital for us to make that human connection, to show him not only our grief but our strength as well. He needed to see the seriousness in our resolve to bring Hanna home.

We also were eager to lay eyes on him. We needed to get some sort of reading on him, witness his mannerisms and get a feel for his personality. The call had to be video. Otherwise, Ahmed would remain a faceless name behind a phone screen.

We'd also sent a list of questions we had for the lawyer ahead of time, and we were anxious to hear the answers. So much seemed to be riding on this call. If this didn't pan out—then what? Where would that leave us?

During the call, for the most part, Amir translated, and there were long periods of time when Tracy and I sat listening to the two men converse in Arabic, not knowing the whole of what was passing between them. At other times, Ahmed spoke to us directly in broken English.

Seeing Ahmed face to face felt like a relief in itself, though we ultimately turned off the video functions in an attempt to improve the call quality. The conversation was going well. We were getting to know this man at last, and we were learning more information about Hanna's case than we'd had in days. While some was admittedly distressing, the overall feeling was a bit like stepping into the light for the first time since hearing the news early Monday morning.

Ahmed advised us again on the intricacies of his worries about putting pressure on the local authorities. It was easier for us to see his genuine concern. It did not seem that he was a conman playing a game but more of a professional carefully considering his strategy and adamant that we all get on the same page and tread carefully for Hanna's sake. His transparency put us more at ease.

We shared the information that a business contact of mine in Egypt had some potentially beneficial connections within the local government of Aghasour, and we discussed how we might utilize that connection to get Hanna into a more comfortable and safer situation while she awaited her next court date. We discussed the best ways to expedite the lab results that were so important for that next hearing. Finally, it seemed like the wheels of this broken-down machine were beginning to turn.

Still, there was one major item we'd yet to cover, and it was a sensitive one. Through all the trust we were building, the one thing still shaking my resolve was the issue of Ahmed's bill. Namely, whether we could trust him to not take it and run.

"He wants the entire 250 now," Amir relayed. Two hundred and fifty thousand Egyptian pounds upfront. I swallowed a lump in my throat.

"He wants everything paid upfront now—250?" I repeated to be sure.

"Yes, that is what he said, Jon," Amir confirmed.

Around sixteen thousand dollars in total. Of course, in my heart, I knew we'd pay anything to bring Hanna home safely— Tracy had brought that reality home when she'd said to me that morning that she'd sell the house if that was what it took. My concern was that Ahmed knew that too.

I stalled for a moment, letting the silence weigh in on the situation, letting Ahmed know that this was a significant request, but I also knew I had to proceed with caution. I knew what I needed to say next but felt as though my words, if not phrased correctly, could throw all our progress off track.

"Okay, just a question," I began. "This is very difficult for me to ask, okay?"

"Feel free," Ahmed insisted, speaking to me directly.

"Please, it is a little bit sensitive, so please don't get mad. In the US, we would do things kind of differently. We would kind of pay as we go, so this . . ." I stalled again to let Ahmed know I was struggling with how to properly frame my question. "We've only just met you. We are only just getting to know you. I don't ask this question to insult you, so again, please don't get mad—"

"Talk to me as if I am your son," Ahmed cut in abruptly.

I let out a nervous laugh. "Okay, so my question is . . . if I give you the whole amount, how do I know for sure you will still work very hard for Hanna?"

There it was. My main concern on the table.

Ahmed began to converse at length with Amir in Arabic. I waited on the edge of my seat to hear how he'd taken my question and how he'd ultimately answer. Everything moving forward seemed to hinge on being able to trust his next response.

The gist of it was this: Ahmed assured us he was dedicated to the case. By this time, he felt moved to bring Hanna home to her family. In fact, when he'd originally traveled to Aghasour to see Hanna, the initial transfer of the money Taylor, Amir, and the others had pooled to retain him hadn't even gone through. He'd gone ahead anyway on faith that it would.

He couldn't argue that he was asking us for a large sum of money; there was no getting around that. But the Egyptian justice system worked differently than ours. He'd have to focus solely on Hanna's case, and there'd be middlemen to pay for various things along the way. He needed the money, yes, but we just had to trust he was sincere.

I didn't have much time to think on it, so I had to go with my gut.

"Okay, Ahmed. Okay," I began. "Let me say this: we are all one team now. It is almost like we are family now. Ahmed, you said Hanna is like your sister, and I believe you. We're all in this together. We have a deal. You'll have the 250 now, and . . ." I paused, making a decision in my mind. ". . . you know what, I will pay you an extra one hundred the moment you send me a picture of Hanna at the airport, ready to leave. Your reward for caring for Hanna." I paused again to make sure my offer was sinking in. "You have my word, Ahmed. As you said to me, God is our witness."

God is our witness. That was one thing Ahmed kept repeating during our conversation—"God is my witness." I wanted him to know that God was witnessing this conversation.

"This is it, Ahmed," I said with finality. "I will pay you 250 now for doing all the work you need to do to get Hanna out. No more, no less. When Hanna is out of there, when she's on her way home, I'll pay you an extra one hundred for getting the job done. Agreed?"

Ahmed agreed.

I could hear the surprise in Ahmed's voice at the promise of the extra money, and though he kept insisting that his motivations were not strictly financial, I could hear the excitement my offer had drummed up as well. Of course, that was why I had made it. I needed to close the door on further negotiations, eliminate the temptation for Ahmed to tack on "expenses" at every turn.

In the end, we had a deal.

When we got off the call, I sat back in my chair and let out the breath I felt I'd been holding for days.

Not all the news on the call had been positive. Ahmed and Amir shared with us that Hanna's arrest had made a local tabloid. Learning this had made my heart jump into my throat; we were horrified. But Ahmed had assured us this wasn't a publication anyone took seriously. "No one reads it," he had said. Still, he thought we should see the photos.

Amir had messaged them over during the call, and I had dismissed them at the time, needing to remain focused on the conversation at hand. Now that Tracy and I were alone, absorbing the weight of everything we had learned and easing into a sense of accomplishment after days of treading water, I picked up my phone and clicked on the article.

Seven men looking smug in their best suits and ties stood boastfully around a table under the glow of harsh fluorescent lights. In front of them, a dozen or so Ziploc bags and a handful of unidentifiable items were lined up meticulously across the table's surface. They were marked in Sharpie and filled with what we, of course, knew to be Hanna's supplements.

There was one large bag that even from the photo we were quick to identify. We had learned from Taylor that Hanna had ordered some high-protein pancake mix just before leaving for Egypt. Of course, we knew what we were looking at because of that information—a big bag of pancake mix. To someone who didn't have that bit of background knowledge, that pancake mix was just a big bag of white powder.

The way the pride shone in the eyes of those men, I knew this was bad. I felt sick to my stomach. This sure looked like it had raised the profile of Hanna's arrest. Those men weren't going to just throw up their hands and admit defeat—*sure, it's just vitamins and breakfast foods.* They would do whatever it took to prove they'd been right all along. I had a feeling that saving face would be more important than the truth to men like that.

"What is it?" Tracy inquired when I let out an exclamation of disbelief, dropping my head into the palm of one hand.

I handed her the phone and tried to recall Ahmed's assurance that no one had seen this. I hoped Hanna never would.

"Jon . . ." Tracy murmured beside me, still looking at my phone. Her fingers were pinching and pulling at the screen, zooming in on the photos. I thought she was about to cry, and I felt the need to reassure her that it was nothing, that we should forget it and move on, but when she looked up at me, she was smiling.

"Jon, that's *my* handwriting on those bags! *I helped her fill these bags! This proves it!* Remember? I helped Hanna pack."

And with that, plan B was born.

TRACY

Hanna procrastinates on packing up until the last minute every single time she travels. She plans months in advance, daydreaming about every minute of her next big adventure, excitedly bending our ears to her plans every chance she has. But when it comes to actual preparedness, packing is inevitably a mad dash with Hanna haphazardly collecting her things in a frazzled and frantic state. While I'd love for her to outgrow this habit and learn to be more proactive with the important details when it comes to her never-ending wanderlust, I have to admit, I always look forward to packing with her, as I'm usually called in to help.

Hanna's trip to Egypt was no exception. Her room—the childhood room she'd spent nine months reinhabiting during the pandemic—looked like a bomb had gone off. Clothes everywhere—on the floor, on the bed, coming out of drawers. Piles of personal belongings she planned to take along for her year abroad.

I stood in her doorway and wondered how she'd manage it all. I already knew—*not without me*. I smiled, imprinting her face, her presence, into my memory—a token to hold on to until she returned home—as she struggled with an armful of boxes and containers before dumping them onto her bed. A bottle of capsules rattled as it fell onto the floor, rolling until it came to rest at my feet. I leaned down and picked it up. *Melatonin*. A brand-new bottle her dad had given her a few weeks back.

"Need some help with this?" I asked, and I saw my daughter startle briefly before registering my presence in her room. She'd been so absorbed in her task she hadn't known I was watching. That moment was mine to keep.

I held the bottle out to her, and she took it.

"Yeah, actually," she said with a wide grin, wiping actual sweat from her brow. "That would be great!"

She contemplated the bottle I'd handed over, then frowned at the large pile of others on her bed. "I need to condense all this stuff somehow. The packaging takes up way too much room, and it's not like I can fit a year's worth into a pill organizer."

I considered the spread and briefly wondered whether she needed it at all. Of course, making that point would be futile.

"Whatever you do, you need to label them," I advised. "I'm not sure how else you're going to keep all this straight."

"Great idea!" she exclaimed and darted from the room.

She returned a moment later carrying a box of Ziploc bags from the kitchen; a permanent marker; and, remarkably, more bottles and bags of supplements. *Would this girl even need food in Egypt?*

As we packed, we talked about her trip. The panic of the last-minute packing spree subsided, and I witnessed the joy and anticipation return as Hanna spoke about her plans. Perfectly in line with Hanna's nature, her agenda for her time abroad included more than just sightseeing and tourist checklists.

Our kids were always passionately involved in our local community, always active in whatever causes and projects I was engaged in. Hanna took a particular liking to that involvement. She served on the youth council, focusing on issues such as homelessness and accessibility to healthy foods and supporting programs against the rising methamphetamine epidemic. Hanna has a passion for getting involved in her local community and a heart for doing good—she always has.

Unfortunately, her passion for travel hasn't always fostered her other interests, and her desire to be involved with her community in a meaningful way is one of those that often took a back seat. While I've always been supportive of Hanna's love of traveling, I was concerned about the void it was creating in her changemaker heart.

It seemed this yearlong trip to Egypt might finally present the opportunity to intertwine her two loves at last. As I meticulously wrote the names of each supplement and herbal remedy onto individual Ziplock bags, I soaked in Hanna's enthusiasm and borderline delirium as she recited all the ways she planned to get involved in her new Egyptian home. She'd put her diving certification to good use cleaning up the coral reef in the Red Sea and working with locals in educating tourists on safe and responsible diving practices. She'd join initiatives to address litter on the beaches and find ways to bond with the locals, officially making them her neighbors.

My heart was heavy in that moment. As a parent, you want your kids to spread their wings and fly, but watching them go is as much full of sorrow as it is pride. As I labeled the last bag, I took another look around her room while she buzzed about, folding and cramming things into her suitcase. Kaya emerged from a pile of clothes she'd been buried under in the chaos, sending them tumbling to the floor in disarray.

I imagined walking past this room tomorrow after Hanna's departure and finding it empty—strike that, finding it *orderly*—for the first time in nearly a year. I chuckled to myself at the thought. Okay, maybe I was ready after all.

Back in my home office, I held Jon's phone, enlarging the photo from the tabloid as much as I could and scrutinizing the bags. Though I couldn't make out the words on each one, I knew without a doubt that those illegible scrawls were in *my handwriting*.

On our call, Ahmed had asked us if we knew what items had been found in Hanna's bags. I'd already begun working with the supplements company to get a list of ingredients for each item Hanna might have taken with her to help the laboratory, but this . . . I looked up to find Jon staring at me, waiting for me to elaborate.

"That's *my* handwriting, Jon," I said. "I labeled each one. I'm sure I can work to identify each supplement and testify as to what it is. I packed them."

That photo, which the authorities grinning slyly back at me from had thought would serve to condemn my daughter, I'd use as my weapon in my fight to free her.

HANNA

From Hanna's Journal
   MY TOOTHBRUSH ARRIVED!!!
   What a difference one hour can make. An hour ago, I felt like I was at my lowest low. Then, they brought me a toothbrush, and we had fish for dinner. I never knew it could feel so good to brush my teeth. Thank God.
   Thank God.

JON

With Tracy's revelation about the tabloid photos, the wheels really started turning in our minds. We were putting everything into place to expedite the lab results, but it was an aggressive timeline. By our count, we were down to thirteen days. Ahmed had mentioned it normally took the lab several weeks—as many as thirty to forty-five days.

Expediting the lab results was our number one focus. It was a huge task; it meant we had to move mountains to set a record. We simply couldn't be sure we'd have them by March 10. And what then? Some system they have—prove that you are innocent, and until then, just rot in prison.

So, plan B was born: to connect the baggies from the photo with the original packaging of the capsules or pills they contained. Visual proof!

Tracy worked tirelessly the remainder of the day to begin identifying what was in each bag. There were a couple that had apparently been added that Hanna had purchased during her three-week stay in Holland. And then there was that huge bag of pancake mix that one of the officers was so proudly pointing at. Taylor had been able to confirm that it was pancake mix because, by a stroke of luck, Hanna had used Taylor's computer, and Taylor was able to access information on what all she had been purchasing.

We would prove that Tracy helped pack the other items and could certify that she knew what was in them. Just supplements, food items, and over-the-counter health products. Could that help our case? We decided not to wait to find out. We were going for it and truly leaving no stone unturned.

I communicated further with my colleague in Egypt and filled him in on what we knew about the case and our conversation with Ahmed. Following Ahmed's advice, I asked him to focus his influence on speeding up the lab results. Coincidentally, a friend of Tracy's reached out to connect us with a man—an Egyptian man—who happened to be familiar with the supplements industry and could help translate if needed.

After days of uncertainty and progress being made at the pace of a slow drip, it was as if the floodgates had opened. We watched messages pour in from family and friends. Hanna was covered in prayer, good thoughts, and heartfelt hope from all corners of the world. My Indian friend, Rajiv, told me his wife was going to temple every day to pray for Hanna. Everywhere we turned, there was someone offering their hand.

At the end of the day, we watched a full moon rise, and for the first time in a week, Hanna didn't feel quite so out of reach.

If there were any good days in all this, Thursday had been a good day. God was connecting people to do good.

FRIDAY, FEBRUARY 26TH

HANNA

From Hanna's Journal
   Am I a good person?
   I'm not sure. If we're a direct reflection of those who surround us, I must be. Everyone in my life is, quite frankly, spectacular. Truly amazing humans. So that must say something about me.
   Right?

———

In jail, where the unfathomable seems to be the norm, a lot can happen in a short period of time. As I prepared for bed Thursday night—brushing my teeth (again, thank God) and enjoying a belly full of fish instead of stale bread and cheese—the cell door flung open, and the guards dumped a mess of a woman into the cell. And I do mean *dumped*. She stumbled in with such force that she fell to the floor as the door slammed shut behind her.

It's not unusual for people to come and go in here, so we all merely paused to take in the sight of her—shaking, struggling to get to her feet. I barely paused the back-and-forth motion of my toothbrush to give notice to her entrance. But when she failed to pick herself up after what was clearly too long, it became apparent that something wasn't right.

It turned out that our new cellmate was severely disabled. A few of us broke free from our disrupted routines to help, noticing as we lifted her to her feet that not only was her shaking uncontrolled (I presumed an advanced stage of something like Parkinson's), but she was wearing adult diapers.

How is someone like this expected to care for herself in such a place?

Tensions ran high, as they always did when new women were added to our already overcrowded accommodations. Our total was now twenty, and sleeping space—not to mention air to breathe—was no longer available to everyone at once. But what began as annoyance naturally melted away into disbelief and empathy as, once again, the true nature of those women revealed itself.

Those women, who had been labeled by society as criminals, knew what was in store the moment we saw the diapers. Did we honestly expect that the guards would come to aid when this poor woman inevitably soiled herself? No, of course we didn't. And so, we took the woman in, just as they'd done for me days earlier, and took turns caring for her throughout the night. When morning came, I had the overwhelming sense that we were all better for it.

It could've easily been every woman for herself in that horrid place, but it wasn't. The compassion the others had for one another was astounding.

The feeling of camaraderie juxtaposed with the degrading reality of our conditions made the idea of Inara leaving soon a next-to-unbearable thought on Friday morning. Though I was settling in, carving out my place among the others, Inara felt like the glue keeping me connected.

I longed for a translation book, something to help me better communicate with the others once she was gone. Even with her there, I couldn't easily partake in group discussions, laugh at jokes being told, or hold a meaningful conversation. I've always craved community, sought it out wherever I've traveled and in every place I've called home. In many ways, Inara was my community. What would I have when she left?

Myself.

As much as I have always longed for connection, I'm also a fiercely independent person. It is a point of pride for me, and I've always felt that it is a major part of my identity. But being independent ultimately means taking care of yourself—being there for yourself. And how quickly that all seemed to crumble when it came down to it.

Faced with my impending isolation, I saw then that there was much work to be done. And maybe God was giving me the space to do it.

"Are you okay?" Inara's voice broke my concentration. I hadn't realized I'd been deep in prayer until just then.

"I'm fine. Why?" I asked.

"You're crying," she replied, then reached out to take my hand. She squeezed it and smiled that smile I knew I'd soon be missing intensely. I tried to reflect her smile back to her.

"I'm fine."

I'll be fine.

TRACY

Days were melting together; we were lost in our work. Thursday had been full of activity. The phone call with Amir and Ahmed had left us energized and with a renewed sense of direction. Since my Facebook post the day before, prayers had been pouring in from every angle. People were eager to help—we just had to ask.

We'd gone to bed late that night—actually, early Friday morning—unable to reconcile the idea of Hanna in the place she was but feeling better than we had so far.

On Friday, Jon sent a message to Ahmed to tell him about our new plan—plan B, as we were already calling it. We had to have a backup plan. Ahmed had told us the day before that in most cases, lab results take up to forty-five days. It was simply unthinkable to imagine Hanna sitting in jail for that long. The sense of despair I felt just thinking of my daughter and what she was enduring . . . We had to do absolutely everything possible to prevent the situation from dragging on that long. How could she possibly survive that?!

Plan A, of course, was relying on receiving the lab results prior to the court hearing. Plan B started on Thursday. I'd had a meeting with the CEO of the supplement company of the products that Hanna was carrying. The news of what was happening to Hanna hit them hard—they were shocked and horrified.

I was deeply humbled by their response. They dropped everything to help document what might be needed for her defense. They gave detailed ingredient lists to help with any lab questions.

They staged products for pictures that I could use to help identify the capsules. They were absolutely incredible.

I spent Friday closely analyzing the tabloid photos and documenting everything I could. We'd enlarged and printed the photos so I could make out the names of various supplements I'd scrawled in my own handwriting.

When I finally looked up from my desk, I was surprised to find the sun already gone and the moon in its place.

"I might have good news," Jon said as he entered my office.

I rubbed at my temples and tried to reconcile the passing of a full day.

"Ibrahim talked with Ahmed," Jon continued. Ibrahim was Jon's business contact in Egypt. He'd been emailing with him about Hanna's case since Tuesday. "He's going to do everything he can to help speed up the lab results. He's taking this matter as a priority. He's already talked with Ahmed. He knows the governor there. He said he'll get back to me after the weekend with an update."

He stood silent for a moment, shaking his head with a look of awe on his face. "It's incredible. I am so grateful for his help. He barely knows me."

I looked down. There were a couple of baggies I had yet to identify. A warm feeling of gratitude came over me. It was heartwarming how people were stepping up and helping in ways we could never have imagined.

Other cases may take forty-five days, but this one wouldn't. Hanna's case was not like any other case. I could feel it with every message that caused my phone to vibrate on my desk, with every email that dinged in my inbox.

We were not alone.

SATURDAY, FEBRUARY 27TH

HANNA

From Hanna's Journal
   The day finally came. The one I've been praying for but dreading all the same. Inara is free.
   I will miss her dearly, but honestly, I'm surprised that I don't feel as taken down by this as I thought I might. Her case is giving me hope. To see her walk out and know she won't be coming back reminded me that I too will be walking out of here. Hopefully soon.
   This isn't forever.

———◆———

Inara left with several other girls, and we all seemed to hold our breath while we waited for news. As much as we were happy to see Inara free, we were scared for one of the others, Zairah, worried her father might be waiting to kill her when she arrived home. He'd found out she had slept with a man before marriage, and when she was done serving her time here, we worried he had his own punishments lined up. Payment for the shame she had brought upon her family. As bad as our conditions were in jail, it was hard to fathom that some might be safer there than at home.

We hugged them and cheered for them as they left, and I gave Inara some letters I had written for my friends and family. When the cell door closed behind them, the atmosphere shifted into a quiet stillness, filled with anxious anticipation.

Finally, word came that Zairah was safe. I cannot describe the light this brought to our day. We could have been envious, could have sat there resenting the other girls and their freedom, could have even wished they were still there to share in our misery. But instead, their absence seemed to bring us all back to life. Twenty-three days Inara had been here. And now, she was free. It gave me hope for March 9.

I spent the afternoon planning all I would do when I was free. I imagined going to Inara and spending an evening together. We'd enjoy a proper meal, sleep in comfortable beds away from the cigarette smoke and the yelling and the cement walls. We'd talk as friends, not cellmates.

I didn't think it was possible to have a good day in that cell until then.

With only seven of us remaining, there was room to stretch. For the first time in days, I felt like moving. Not just transitioning from standing to sitting to lying down but actually *moving*. I could already feel my muscles withering away from the lack of exercise.

I took advantage of the space and began to stretch. Soon, others were joining me, and before I knew it, we were synced in a steady flow, working our way through sun salutations. I'd been meditating as a way to connect with God and find peace within myself for days, but in that moment, I felt the most profound connection with the other women. I was sore and out of practice, but every movement was deeply healing. Occasionally, one of us would lose our balance and fall, and the room would erupt in laughter. It felt so good to laugh.

In the evening, we received another blessing—specifically, I had received a blessing in the form of pizza. Not just enough for me but for everyone. I was confused at first; I could only assume the pizza was from Ahmed—who else?—but the confusion did not matter at the moment. I was grateful for the opportunity to provide something. To contribute something.

Savoring my slice of pizza, I looked around the circle as we all sat together for a meal. The mood was lighter than it had been since the night I'd arrived, and though the room buzzed with conversation I could not understand, for a moment, I forgot all about the language barrier between me and those women. When it comes down to it, our energy all speaks the same language.

As night fell, the women began to settle in. We reorganized our belongings and spread out our blankets, grateful for the opportunity to space out. For the first time in many nights, we all had room to lie down at once. Everyone was looking forward to a good night's sleep.

Down the hall, in the men's block, all was quiet except for a single voice. We lay still in the dark while the beautiful song of a faceless man sang us all to sleep.

As the music filled my ears and my body and mind slowly loosened their grip on the waking world, it never once occurred to me that I could not understand the words.

JON

With every day that passed, our focus on plan B intensified. Every morning, we woke both grateful to be one day closer to March 10 and terrified by the very real possibility that we wouldn't have the information we needed to support Hanna in court when the day arrived. Still, we never waited for answers. We plowed ahead, exploring every opportunity that presented itself in our path.

Being across the world was, of course, not ideal. It left us feeling helpless, out of control. But after discussing it at length with Ahmed, we made the difficult decision to not travel to Aghasour. Ahmed highly advised against it. The last thing we wanted was to draw unnecessary scrutiny upon Hanna's case by showing up in Aghasour, demanding answers and attention.

But we couldn't leave Hanna on her own either. Saturday, I began making arrangements with Taylor. We had twelve days until court. While we prayed for a miracle—and it was pretty clear that's what it would take—we knew the odds were not in our favor for getting Hanna home that day. Someone needed to be with Hanna when the verdict was delivered. Someone needed to be there in person to lend her strength.

Her younger sister—despite all their differences and the sibling rivalry that had followed them through childhood and into their relationship as adults—took on the responsibility without hesitation. While Hanna has always been our dreamer, Taylor is our doer. Her ability to evaluate, plan, and execute accordingly hardly ever fails to amaze us.

I'll admit I wasn't thrilled with the idea of Taylor landing in the same country that had just swallowed our other daughter whole. But working as a team meant trusting as a team, and I knew Taylor was up to the task. Plus, she'd be accompanied by her boyfriend, Erik, and Ahmed would be expecting their arrival. I kept the image of Taylor and Hanna reunited at the forefront of my mind as we looked at airline tickets and hotels.

We had a solid team, and that filled our hearts with immense gratitude. That morning, we received a message from Amir.

Hello, everyone. I am flying to Aghasour today. I hope to see Hanna soon.

As we learned more about the conditions Hanna was living in, we were horrified to hear that the jail provided very little in the way of sustenance. The women depended on their family, friends, or lawyers to deliver food and personal items, and those were the lucky ones. The less fortunate were left to rely on the kindness and generosity of their cellmates. Originally, we'd been under the impression Hanna was receiving care packages daily from Ahmed's junior attorney, but we were to learn later on that this wasn't the case.

Hearing that Amir, one of our own, would soon be with our daughter brought us great relief. We arranged for him to provide some items that would not only fill her stomach but also her time. Thinking back to the one letter we'd seen scribbled haphazardly on a torn piece of paper bag, we all agreed that a proper journal might bring Hanna some comfort.

Though we continued to work from the confines of our home office and kitchen table, the unfathomable distance between us and our daughter seemed to be shrinking.

SUNDAY, FEBRUARY 28TH

TRACY

Much like working with any government agency, dealing with the US Embassy was a dreadfully slow process. Taylor called them again on Sunday to inquire about what, if anything, was being done. The initial relief she felt when she was finally able to get someone on the phone was quickly replaced with frustration.

"They said they still haven't received the privacy release form," she recounted to us, her voice tired and fraught with disbelief. I could picture this pragmatic daughter of mine, thousands of miles away in her Amsterdam apartment, pacing by the window with strain chiseled in her face at what she surely perceived was the incompetence she was up against. "So, I sent it *again*."

She's a real matter-of-fact, get-'er-done kind of person, always striving for perfection. We were on the phone with her finalizing the details of her trip to Egypt. She'd booked a flight, and Jon was in the process of reserving a hotel room.

We had few details of Hanna's case to catch each other up on, and the turtle's pace at which the bureaucratic side of things seemed to be moving was less than encouraging. The conversation turned to how Taylor's role, more than anything once she arrived in Aghasour, would be to provide strength for her Hanna. Strength given the increasingly likely scenario that Hanna would not be traveling home with her after court.

Not for the first time in this ordeal, I was struck by Taylor's steadfastness—her dedication to her sister. And not just hers, for that matter. Throughout the day, we were communicating with Amir. The police weren't letting him see Hanna, which was disappointing and confusing given that Ahmed was supposed to have had this cleared.

When Amir had arrived on Saturday, he had brought pizza for Hanna and enough for everyone in the cell to share, which was apparently custom. But all he could do was drop it off at the police station and leave. They wouldn't let him see Hanna.

On Sunday, he had tried again, delivered more items. And yet again, he had been turned away from seeing her. He decided to extend his trip and called in a last-ditch-effort favor with a relative who was in the military special services.

We waited for good news.

And then, we received some. Ahmed had texted us a picture of a letter.

Mom and Dad—

I'm not sure how to start this letter because I'm not sure how to express my deep and utter sorrow. I can only imagine the pain and fear I have caused you. Since here, I've realized a lot of things I need to give proper attention—beginning with my selfishness. Although this situation is a huge accident and not intentional, it doesn't take away the light shone on some issues I need to work on. I promise you both that

I will overcome my shortfalls and I will never put you through this or anything like it again. True to my nature, I will come out of this awful situation stronger, wiser, and closer to my biggest support (aside from the two of you), God. I told you I've experienced the power of prayer for the first time here, and it continues to bring me strength. My time with God provides me peace, but I'm also asking to be shown the way. What is He trying to show me? What do I need to open myself to?

These last seven days have been life changing. I've witnessed atrocious things and am living in a grim environment. No one should have to live like this. The thing is I know it could be worse, and I've faced my privilege and blessings like never before. Outside of prayer, I have an absolutely incredible support system here. Each girl looks out for the others with so much compassion and care. These girls pick me up when I go down and vice versa. These girls have some of the best hearts I've ever witnessed. We have cared for the mentally ill, the severely disabled. We've seen each other through emotional breakdowns and prayed together. We all share the little we have with one another and continue to give each other hope. I wrote to you before about Inara, who speaks some English. She'll leave tomorrow and hopefully get you this letter. I'll be sad to see her go, but I know I will be okay until my next court date.

I don't want to sugarcoat the situation or conditions here, but I do want to tell you guys I'm being cared for by amazing ladies and Ahmed, my lawyer. I also feel your love and support each and every day. I am using this time to be better. I will get through this as a better person.

I love you.

Sometimes, when you're waiting for the news you think you need, you end up receiving the news you needed most.

HANNA

From Hanna's Journal
Another day down.
*I've now been here as many days as I have until my next court
date. Until my hopeful release. I'm trying not to dwell on all the things
that could go wrong. I know I have many people fighting hard for me
on the outside, but in here, it is all out of my hands.*
*Today, I am emotionally okay but physically ill. Still, it is so nice
to have space to stretch out.*
*I can't help wondering whether my letter made it to Mom and
Dad or when I might hear back. But for now, I am comfortable, and
that is all that matters.*

———

As I sat writing, a guard appeared at the cell door and called my
name. When I looked up, pen poised over the ever-shrinking blank
space on what remained of the tattered paper bag, my eyes landed
on the collection of items he held in his arms.

"For . . . me?" I asked, my voice catching in my throat.

He raised his eyebrows impatiently, proffering the items out
toward me. I rose hesitantly to my feet while the other women
stared on. As I took the armful of items, I could feel the glances
darting between them.

Returning to my space, I took inventory of this unexpected delivery. It seemed Inara had come through for me. Snacks and fresh fruit. *Fresh fruit!* Apples, bananas, oranges. In my mind, I was already calculating how long I could make it last. Gratitude and excitement swelled in my chest, and my hands shook as I gripped an Arab to English translation guide and two notebooks. All those pages—lined, blank pages—waiting to be filled.

"Fals," a voice above me said, and I looked up to see two of the women standing before me.

"What?" I questioned, having recognized the word. One of the only words I knew so far. Money.

"Fals," the woman repeated and pointed to Obaida.

Before Inara had left, she'd insisted I give all of the money I had left to Obaida, whom I can only describe as being the "cell boss."

"How much you have left?" she'd asked quietly, nodding to the pocket of my jacket where I kept my money.

I shrugged.

"A bit." I'd been trying to conserve it, wanting to make it last as long as possible. I'd bought water and cigarettes for bartering.

Inara had looked around the cell then, the worry on her face making me feel suddenly uneasy.

"Let Obaida hold it for you," she'd said at last, making up her mind. "I think that is better."

I was confused, but I didn't argue it. Did she think I'd be safer without the cash on me? For all the support she'd been providing to me emotionally, I guess I'd never considered how she might be protecting me physically.

With Inara now gone and not a lick of English spoken among the remaining girls, it was difficult to understand how the system worked. So, when the items were delivered that day, it caused some confusion. As best as I could understand, I was meant to purchase the things I'd received from Obaida. That, of course, was just an assumption. I had no clue what was actually going on. "Fals, fals," they kept repeating at me while chattering amongst themselves urgently. All the commotion was going to my head.

I threw my hands up in surrender.

"Fine. Fine. Whatever, just . . ." I said, trying to make them understand I was beyond caring. I just wanted a moment to enjoy the comfort of the gifts I'd received. ". . . fine." I spoke the last word as calmly as I could but with finality, nodding in agreement.

As they walked away, I returned my attention to the notebooks in my lap. I set the first aside, and my breath caught in my chest as my eyes focused on the cover of the second notebook. The face of a woman stared back at me, her chin tilted up, her jaw set, her gaze a determined and steady stare. Arrows were slung across her back, and over her heart, she held one tightly clenched fist.

Beneath the sketch—*Sagittarius*.

How would Inara have known? This couldn't have been a random coincidence.

As I lifted the journal to examine the woman—the warrior—more closely, a note slipped from behind the cover and fluttered to the floor before me. I reached for it.

I recognized his handwriting instantly.

Stay strong.

MONDAY, MARCH 1ST

HANNA

From Hanna's Journal
   First entry in a real notebook.
   I am very tired today, trying to fight off this head cold I've come down with. Mayi woke me in the early hours, asking me to scoot over so she could make her bed next to mine. At first, I was confused—why did she need to be SO close to me?—but then I realized more women had joined us in the night. So, I guess we're back to squeezing in.
   That's how quickly circumstances can change here. Things are starting to look grim again, but I haven't cried yet today, and so far, I've cried every day.
   That's something, isn't it?

———

I reset myself with a nap, which was fairly easy to do with the congestion and the unrelenting headache contributing to my exhaustion.

I had the strangest dream. In it, champagne glasses clinked together as I toasted with a childhood friend, Ben, at some swanky affair. It was a party celebrating a fancy new weed shop he was opening (not surprising, as that is his business now in LA), and emotions were flowing. I felt light. There was laughter and dancing. Ben's smile was warm. We turned away from the crowd, and I found we were high up on a hill. Below us, the pyramids of Cairo rose majestically from the earth. Their presence was staggering, but they felt impossibly far away.

I awoke in such high spirits, I went immediately to my new journal. I needed to record exactly what I was feeling, but I didn't even quite know what to write. Had something happened in my case, or was God simply providing me with the second wind I needed that day? All I knew was something had changed. Something *had* happened. *I could feel it.*

TRACY

Thank you so much, Ben. We really appreciate your help.

I sent the message and set my phone down.

"Ben came through," I related as Jon entered my office, offering a mug of coffee.

"He did? That's wonderful!"

I'd reached out to Ben regarding one of the items I'd been having difficulty identifying from the tabloid photos. The substance hadn't come from the same supplements company as the rest, and we'd determined it to be a CBD probiotic based on a sheer stroke of luck the day before.

When we'd received Hanna's letter, there had been a note scribbled in the margins. Like us, she had clearly spent a lot of time considering what she'd had in her possession. She was sure it should all be fine; everything was over the counter and easily explained away. But there was one substance giving her pause—the CBD. Legally purchased in Idaho, the probiotic was still a marijuana-derived product. As quickly as the worry had arisen that that could pose a problem, I had heard Hanna's exasperated voice in the back of my mind.

"They're not *drugs*, Mom. It's not even close to the same thing as pot. It just comes from the same plant."

Still, I couldn't help but wonder. Would this be an issue in a less forward-thinking country like Egypt?

I knew more than most might about a variety of illicit and illegal substances through establishing an anti-drug coalition and chairing the Association Cities Drug Task Force. But admittedly, I didn't know enough about CBD products to be confident approaching this issue on an international level. So, I reached out to someone I knew could help.

One of Hanna's oldest friends, Ben, was involved in the CBD oil business out in California. I knew they hadn't been close recently—merely the side effects of friendship at a distance—and I didn't even know if he was aware of her trip. Breaking the news of what had happened wasn't going to be easy, but I knew Ben would do anything to help. Turns out, Hanna has that effect on people.

I was right. Ben would have been willing to go to the ends of the Earth to help our girl. In fact, minutes into our conversation, I had to talk him down from doing just that, as he was ready to jump on a plane and fly to Egypt. We were still in the middle of a pandemic, after all, and Amir was even having a hard time convincing the police to let him see her. But there was one way he could help Hanna.

"They're simple CBD supplements—shouldn't be an issue at all." I got Jon up to speed while I typed out the details I'd just secured into the document I'd been compiling for plan B.

Since we'd received the letter the day before, Jon had been reading up on the legality of CBD oil and supplements in Idaho, and Ben's confirmation further solidified our strategy. Hanna was fully within her rights to have CBD in Idaho, and as far as we could tell, she was free to travel with it as well.

Aside from the unidentified powder the authorities had claimed was cocaine—and the origins of which had not been made clear—that left one baggie of little white pills left to identify. I'd been having difficulty with that one, and the supplement company didn't recognize them either. Our options for identification were dwindling, and our hopes were now resting on Hanna. We'd sent Amir with the photo. If Hanna could tell us what they were, we could do the rest.

But Amir still needed to get in a room with her. According to his latest messages, he was giving it one last shot tonight.

HANNA

From Hanna's Journal
Trust my gut! This is crazy!
Amir came to visit me!

I was caught off guard when they came to pull me from the cell. I understood I had a visitor, but I hadn't been expecting anyone. They hadn't even been allowing me to see Ahmed at the station, but of course, I assumed it had to be him.

When they escorted me into the room and I saw Amir sitting across the table, my legs went wobbly. I sat down, tongue-tied. I could hardly believe it was really him, but of course, it was! It only made sense. All weekend, I'd felt something was different. The food that had been delivered, the items . . . the note. I don't know why I'd assumed he'd just been instructing Inara on what to bring. Of course, he'd picked out the Sagittarius notebook himself. *Of course!*

I was equal parts amazed and horrified. I couldn't believe my luck, and at the same time, I was so ashamed he'd come all this way for me. We were done, had been for a while. And here I was, disrupting his life with this mess. Would I have done the same for him had the roles been reversed? Yes, absolutely yes. But seeing him there, learning how he'd dedicated the past week to helping me—how all my loved ones had—was honestly nausea inducing. Guilt flushed my cheeks and ran through my veins.

But, oh, was it good to see a familiar face. I sat stunned for much of our visit, somehow forgetting all the words I'd been saving up to share with my loved ones the second I had a chance, and let Amir do the talking. It took only moments for the foggy picture of my case to start to clear. All those answers I'd been craving while locked behind those concrete walls—Amir had them. My family was working hard to bring me home, not that I'd ever doubted that. They were working every angle—the State Department, our senator's office at home, the embassy, the supplements!

When Amir shared my parents' plan to identify the items I'd had in my bag, my head swirled with the enormity of the task. *How . . .*

Amir cut my thoughts short, producing an enlarged photo, a close-up of a bag of tiny white pills.

"Your mother," he began, "has been amazing. This is the only one left they have yet t—"

I knew instantly what they were.

"Melatonin!" I shouted, jabbing a finger at the collection of white tablets in a plastic bag. Even from the low-quality photo, I could see the characteristic powdery residue that the tablets left on the inside of the bag. "That's melatonin!"

Amir smiled and nodded, putting the photo away.

"Great. That's great, Hanna. Your parents will be thrilled. Thank you."

"Thank *you*," I said. "Thank you *all*." I don't think I've ever meant anything more in my life.

The short visit was filled with highs and lows. I was devastated—though not surprised— to learn that my parents had canceled their anniversary trip to Mexico.

"Please, please tell them I said they should go," I begged him, though I suspected it was in vain.

"I do have some good news though," he replied, diverting the conversation. "Taylor will be here for your next court date."

I was on the edge of my seat in an instant, eyes filling with tears. I fought them back. I wouldn't cry. I would have *one day* without crying.

"Really?" I gasped. "She's coming *here*?"

"Yes," Amir answered. Then, he quickly rushed to say, "Your parents would come, of course, but . . . there are travel restrictions, and Ahmed doesn't think—"

"No," I interrupted. "No, I understand. But Taylor is coming?" I couldn't believe it. My heart pounded in my chest, full of so much love and gratitude I thought it might burst.

"She'll be here in six days," Amir said. "She hopes to see you before court." A pause as he looked around the room they'd allowed for visitation. I was suddenly very glad he couldn't see the cell from where we sat. He lowered his voice. "How are you, Hanna?"

"I'm good," I nodded enthusiastically and sat up even straighter in my chair. "It's—well, you know . . ." How could I assure him I was really okay given the circumstances? "But I'm strong."

And in that moment, I did feel strong.

———

From Hanna's Journal
Thank you, thank you, thank you, God, for this day.
Another day wrapping up. Everyone is in better spirits again.
Another beautiful serenade from down in the men's block. I can be strong for six more days to see my sister.
It's only a matter of time.

TUESDAY, MARCH 2ND

JON

Things were moving forward. It was astonishing how people were appearing in our path, sometimes as if out of thin air. They were willing and eager to help—to use their personal connections, their time and energy, to aid Hanna. They were all driven by concern and care. Really, they were all driven by love. We accepted it all with open arms.

There were opportunities presented that we were able to take advantage of immediately. On Monday, a friend of Tracy's who had previously been employed with our senator's office managed to get the senator's chief of staff personally engaged in Hanna's case. This felt like a big win for us. This was a man who could use his contacts and the influence of their office as an additional push in our current struggle to get the US Embassy actively involved.

There were other opportunities that came out of left field, things much too convenient to ever be written off as coincidence. Our network was growing and spreading across the globe. We were put in contact with neighbors of relatives living states away—it was humbling. These were people who could help in ways we hadn't seriously considered, ways we honestly hoped to not have to resort to. We had to keep them in our back pocket while carefully considering the potential implications.

Plan A, the original goal of expediting the lab results in time for the court date on March 10, was still in the works, but we were growing increasingly frustrated with the lack of support from the embassy. Hanna's identification of the final substance during her visit with Amir had nicely tied up the last loose end for plan B. The initial stirrings for another contingency, a plan C, were there, but for now, we needed to remain focused on the task at hand.

Working on plan A felt like trying to free a vehicle stuck in the mud when the four-wheel drive was just not kicking in. Ahmed was working hard on Hanna's case and had a meeting set up for Wednesday with the Ministry of Justice to discuss what could be done on the government's side to speed up the lab results.

He had requested, in vain, the support of the US Embassy at the meeting. To our true surprise and disappointment, we received nothing but radio silence from the embassy. We messaged our new contact in the senator's office to see if he could shed light on the situation. His response was disheartening. He did not seem to think the embassy would be involving themselves at this stage.

While preparing for the meeting the next day, Ahmed sent some words of encouragement.

This is what I expected, so don't give up. Don't worry. God will arrange everything, and we will work very, very hard.

Ahmed's confidence was inspiring, but I was not going to let up on the embassy. Ibrahim, my Egyptian business contact, was helping more through his connections with the governor in Aghasour than the official channels were. For all the gratitude I felt toward those who were stepping up, I couldn't help but become more aggravated by those who should but wouldn't.

On Tuesday, I sat down and wrote an email to the embassy. The subject line: "Hanna Willems.'"

Dear sir/madam:

We urgently request contact from the US Embassy.

Our daughter, Taylor Willems, has tried various times throughout the week to talk to someone from the embassy for an update on Hanna. She was reassured Hanna's case information would be shared as soon as the privacy release was received.

She is still unable to make contact with anyone who is on the case and has been told several times she'd be receiving a call back. She has yet to hear anything from anyone at the US Embassy.

We would like to understand why we are being blocked from learning anything about our daughter's case.

Our request is urgent; we are doing everything in our power to get Hanna out of the terrible conditions she is in and are desperate for help from you. Please advise us on what we need to do to make contact with the officer on this case.

Sincerely,

Jon and Tracy Willems

I hit send, not sure what to expect. Maybe my frustration was misplaced. These were also difficult times for the embassy personnel. As tough as it was to remind myself, the world was still spinning throughout our crisis. All US government officials were in the midst of a presidential transition, and COVID was still rampant across the globe.

I took a deep breath. *Trust me, I am here.* Ahmed was right. God would arrange everything.

HANNA

From Hanna's Journal

I woke up sad today and immediately took it as a sign that some-thing bad had happened with my case. I instantly began to cry, but almost just as quickly, I caught myself and threw the negative thoughts away. No, Hanna. No.

I cannot twist the sign God gave me yesterday, waking up elated as I had and knowing that it meant something, and make it mean that every time I feel down, something horrible must be happening. It is okay to be emotional. It is okay to feel sad.

As soon as I started to count my blessings, I felt better.

When I say that my family and friends were the rock providing me a steady foundation during the hardest of days, I mean it. Not only were they the ones moving my case ahead while I sat helpless in jail, but focusing on their love and support helped pull me out of my darkest moments. The more I practiced holding on to that positivity and imagining my freedom, the more fleeting those moments be-came. It was easy to look around the room and see nothing but filth, despair, and injustice, but I kept counting those blessings.

I did not have it bad in a bad situation.

After my visit with Amir, I had returned to the cell feeling as strong as I'd intended to make him believe. I had the most amazing support system someone in my position could hope for. Not many of the women around me could say the same. That night, I prayed for each of them.

Tuesday passed with the blessing of a long stretch of sleep. If I had to guess—and I did have to guess—I'd say I had slept somewhere around ten hours. The day, like many others, was mostly uneventful.

At one point though, the guards arrived suddenly and demanded we cover ourselves and stand. They came in, snorting and spitting, mannerisms I'd come to think were a show meant to intimidate us. All I could understand was something about a phone, something about making calls. I assumed they wanted us to make calls for food. We were nearly out and could only receive deliveries of outside food on Sundays and Thursdays. We would have to settle for bread and sugar water and what little we had left.

I'd love a phone call, I thought as they passed over me. I doubted I would be getting one.

When they left again, I took inventory of the fruit I had left. What could I share? Sharing was not hard. When I had received my delivery days earlier, it would have been easy for the others to turn up their noses at me, jealous of my newly acquired wealth. But aside from the initial confusion around the money, there had been none of that. Instead, they had been happy for me. I'd share what I could that night and hope that one of us would have another delivery soon.

I took a shower and changed into clean clothes. I'd been allowed a few items from my suitcase—what hadn't been confiscated, that is. A clean body and clear mind did a lot to take my thoughts away from my empty stomach. A wave of resolve washed over me.

I could do this.

TRACY

"Here," I said, raising my phone and turning the camera to "selfie" mode. "To show Hanna."

Smiling behind our masks, on a plane bound for Mexico, I snapped the photo of Jon and myself heading off on our anniversary trip as originally planned.

The thought that we had canceled our trip because of her had caused Hanna additional stress and feelings of immense regret. After their visit, Amir had relayed Hanna's wishes that we'd reconsider, though he'd promised her nothing at the time. Everyone expected us to stay, to hold down the fort. Isn't that what people did in times like these?

But when we'd looked around the "fort," what had we found? Hanna wasn't there. None of our contacts were there. Our team wasn't there. We hadn't been doing anything that couldn't be done from anywhere. I had done all I could developing plan B. Getting away could help us focus, think clearly outside the noise of daily tasks.

As Jon had plugged away at efforts with the embassy, I'd packed. We needed to clear our minds. We needed to clear our hearts. A quiet beach in Mexico seemed as good a place as any to do it.

WEDNESDAY, MARCH 3RD

HANNA

From Hanna's Journal

Sleeping all day yesterday came back to bite me, and I didn't sleep at all last night. More time alone with my thoughts. More time to wonder. More time to sit, drowning in guilt and worry.

As the others began to wake up, I was glad for the company. The general mood of the cell had a buzz of excitement around it, as Obaida was supposed to be called to court today. But when the time arrived, no one came for her. The mood in the cell soured immediately.

The exhaustion from the anticipation and letdown was enough to finally allow me to close my eyes and get some sleep.

It wasn't restful.

———

I awoke suddenly to the sound of yelling and the sensation of being jostled and tugged at. My dreams having been as unsettling as reality, it took me more than a moment to realize I was awake and that the other women were barking at me to get up. With the hurried and somewhat forceful help of one of the women, I pulled myself off the ground and shuffled with the flow of bodies toward the cell door. We were like feeder fish trying to avoid a net.

What's going on? My groggy mind reeled.

In the hall, we formed a line, and the guards ordered us to stand with our backs against the wall. I looked around at the faces of the others, trying to glean some sort of understanding of what was going on. Some looked as bewildered as I was; some, just annoyed. A few still held those same despondent expressions they always wore. Business as usual.

Then, the sound of heavy footsteps down the hall. I looked up to find two more guards marching with purpose toward us, and my body stiffened. I was disheveled from sleep, my feet were bare, and even in the heat, I found myself wishing I'd grabbed my jacket or scarf. I wanted to cover up every inch of skin.

When you're locked away in the cell for days on end, losing your sense of self as you sleep huddled against the bodies of women you cannot speak to, no contact with the outside world, you begin to feel anonymous. Invisible. Standing in the hall with those men quickly approaching, I felt painfully visible and on display. I did not want their eyes on me, did not want to be inspected or appraised. I pressed my back to the wall, squeezed in tighter with the others, and wished to form with them that amorphous mass—one body of many faceless women.

And then, the two men walked past us. I let go of the breath I did not know I had been holding.

I sucked it in again—hard—once it became apparent what was happening.

We watched, helpless, from the hallway as these two men entered our cell and began to tear it apart. There was zero regard given to neatly folded stacks of clothes, personal belongings carefully lined up or tucked into pillowcases. Dried, caked clay from their boots littered the floor, and my resentment for this filthy box I'd been caged in for over a week was suddenly and alarmingly over-shadowed by a fierce and unexpected sense of protectiveness.

Without warning, my mind transported me back to those first surreal moments at the airport, watching from across the room as security rifled through my belongings. Those very moments that had landed me where I stood now, barefoot on a dusty concrete floor. Sweat prickled to the surface of my skin. I felt a dizzying sensation as though the world had begun to spin a little too fast and something—what, I didn't know—was perilously close to slipping out of my grasp.

My throat clenched painfully as the beginnings of some sort of protest were strangled and released as nothing more than an aching whimper. My eyes darted around to the other women as if we could somehow band together and stop this—this blatant disrespect for our belongings, for ourselves as human beings.

No one looked as though they were prepared to speak up. I deflated. Then, I returned my gaze to the cell and watched as the ash from one guard's cigarette fell in a slow flurry, leaving traces of charred cheap tobacco over all our few and precious belongings, a smear that would be impossible to erase completely for days to come.

Five days, I told myself. And I gritted my teeth so hard, I feared they might crack.

Once our cell was completely upturned, the guards finally came out, grumbling to each other in words I could not understand, but I could get the gist—whatever they had been looking for, they hadn't found it.

Buoyed by my own anger, my eyes drilled into the men as they passed in frustrated conversation, silently daring them to meet my gaze. But when one of them did, I froze. There was an almost imperceptible pause as he walked by me, close enough for me to smell the stench of sweat and smoke. A cigarette dangled loosely from one corner of his mouth, and the other turned up into a sickening smirk.

Go ahead—do it, his eyes seemed to taunt. He was calling my bluff.

I wanted to scream. "THOSE ARE OUR THINGS! HOW DARE YOU? WE'RE HUMAN BEINGS, NOT RATS IN A CAGE!"

Everything in me wanted to spit in his face. Instead, the saliva pooled in my mouth. Before I could process my own thoughts of what to do next, he reached up slowly, pulling the cigarette from his mouth and releasing a toxic cloud of smoke. Immediately, it filled my lungs and made my eyes burn. I steeled myself against the fit of choking and coughing I knew was coming. I could only hold it back for so long, but even if I could not speak up, I certainly wouldn't give him the pleasure of seeing me break down right in front of him.

As his back disappeared down the hall, I let out a series of smothered gags, still determined not to make a scene of it. When I finally unclenched my fists, I opened them slowly to reveal angry half-moons dug deep into my palms.

Back in the cell—*our cell*, my mind still screamed—we began our attempt at cleanup. With the cell door shut firmly behind us and the guards all back at their usual posts, we were once again invisible. At least we were alone. All at once, the indignation that had been coursing through my body moments earlier gave way to another emotion. Picking up my pillow from the floor, I rubbed my palm furiously at the perfect, dirty imprint of a boot square in its center. It might as well have been on my very own cheek.

All the anger I had been pressing down deep within my core rushed up to my throat and burst out in a flood of sobs and tears as Aaida and I worked wordlessly side by side to straighten our things. As we shook ash from our clothes and refolded them, then divided the personal items that had been tossed carelessly in a heap in the center of the room, I noticed the silent tears streaming down her face. My chest ached as I watched her wipe them away with the back of her wrist and keep on working. How many times had she had her life torn apart like this and said nothing as she pulled it back together?

Not everyone joined in our efforts. Though I tried not to give her attention at first, it was difficult to ignore Mayi meandering around the cell, eyeing the mess that was left and laughing. Always laughing.

I tried to reason with myself whenever Mayi's laugh started to get under my skin. This was clearly a coping mechanism of some sort. I cried. Mayi laughed. Aaida sat in silent despair. Mayi laughed. The pregnant lady shrieked and clawed at the cell door. Mayi laughed.

She doesn't understand. Deep breath in.

She's fighting her own battles. Deep breath out.

But there she stood, laughing, refusing to help as Aaida and I tried to salvage some dignity from the situation, and it only made my tears come faster and harder. Without warning, the laughter took on a tone that felt targeted, personal.

"It's not funny!" I had turned on her before I could even have known I was about to speak.

Everyone stopped and stared. The air turned to a sudden stillness that, in the wake of the day's chaos, seemed unnatural. I was breathing heavy, my chest heaving with each breath as though that one short exclamation had been some sort of athletic feat and I stood anticipating the final score. Like hurling the shot put in front of crowded stands. One go, all your effort. Wait for it to land.

Mayi held her breath for a moment, clearly unsure what to think of my outburst. Then, she snorted, a trickle of giggles escaped, and soon, she was back to full-on laughter. She shook her head and walked away. Still laughing.

My hands shook as I returned to my work, the weight of everyone's stares upon my back.

Wanting to erase the raid on our cell from my mind, I started by attempting to erase all its physical evidence. I washed my pillow and jacket. I couldn't stomach the idea of my face resting against the treads of that man's boots at night or recalling his smoke in my mouth as I inhaled the ash covering my clothing. I scrubbed long and hard, and still, the water ran out brown. I worked at it until my fingers were raisins and the other women's stares made it clear that it was time to give up and move on.

Later, when the cell was practically as it had been before the search, the only thing left to clean up was the uneasiness left in its wake. I watched as, around the cell, the women slowly and quietly fell back into their routines. Soft conversations began to pick up, cigarettes were lit, some gave in to the temptation of sleep to pass the time.

If you've ever thrown a rock into a koi pond, you've seen how the fish scatter and hide. Only minutes later, a few venture out. Soon, all is forgotten, and life in the pond returns to normal. As if rocks aren't falling from the sky.

Looking around the room, I imagined another instance like today happening again tomorrow. Or maybe the next day. Or maybe next week.

How can I live like this?

I turned to Aaida and asked a simple question, hoping she'd understand.

"Why?"

She replied with a single word: "Phone."

Not comprehending at first, I felt my eyes narrow in confusion. Maybe she hadn't understood me after all. Then, she raised her hand in a general sweeping motion across the expanse of the cell, a gesture that seemed to encompass all the other women. Then, I understood. I scanned the room once again, my eyes passing over each of my fellow cellmates. Was it even possible?

Did one of these women somehow have a phone?

JON

We had arrived Tuesday at our resort. Our temporary home away from home was along Costa Mujeres, north of town. It was beautiful, almost serene. And very quiet. Tourism in the area had clearly taken a hard hit from the pandemic, and though we were away from the hustle and bustle of the popular hotel zone, I was wondering how deserted that might be at the moment as well. We practically had the place to ourselves.

Tracy and I had tried to soak it all in, and at first, it really did take the edge off. A photo from our arrival at the resort shows Tracy, her eyes smiling at the camera, toasting the air with a welcome glass of sparkling rosé. It was a momentary reprieve.

After we were settled, we were once again up against this hard edge. This hard, sharp edge of reality. The warm, coastal breeze did what it could to cushion us, but we couldn't escape reality digging in at every uncomfortable angle.

We weren't there to escape anyway. We were there to get some space, to get some fresh air. There was still plenty of work to be done.

On Wednesday evening, I sat down to update our friends and family on our progress.

Here is an update on the activities that are taking place to help get Hanna out of this crisis.

Our attorney, Ahmed, continues to work relentlessly to help Hanna. He had a meeting today with the Ministry of Justice and was able to complete the forms necessary to expedite the lab testing. I have a business associate who is working with his contacts in the ministry as well.

In the meantime, Tracy is pursuing and utilizing her contacts. One of her good friends had a connection with the embassy in Morocco. He provided some insight into what is going on at the US Embassy in Egypt. Here is his note below:

> My contact in Morocco just sent me this:
>
> "I reached out to my counterpart in Cairo. Apparently, this case has received a lot of attention, and they are doing everything they can for her, working through the embassy's legal and procedural processes."
>
> That is certainly good news!
>
> Unfortunately, the legal system is a very slow process, especially over there. However, nothing makes it move faster than shining a spotlight on it, which I believe you have done. I will keep you updated!

It is amazing how people have come together and are acting out of love and care. We are deeply, deeply humbled by how God is leading us in this situation. And He works in mysterious ways and on His timeline, all driven by love and goodness.

HANNA

From Hanna's Journal

I dreamt of my sentencing. Men in cloaks led me down a dark forest path to a small clearing where my loved ones were gathered in a circle, everyone facing away or averting their eyes. No one would meet my gaze. I broke free and ran to my mom, collapsing into her arms, desperately clinging to her. She squeezed me back, and we both began to cry. Finally, my dad looked down at me, his hand coming to rest on my shoulder, soft but firm. I swear I could feel them both. As I met my dad's eyes, he said in a painfully sober voice, a voice that was not quite his own, "Hanna, this will be a punishment you remember forever."

A judge appeared. My parents stood resolutely by my side as all my friends and family joined hands around us. I wasn't given time to speak. The wind rushed through the trees above me as the judge delivered the sentencing: four years.

I turned around in disbelief to find my loved ones ripped from me, disappearing into the dark recesses of the forest. In the clearing remained a single tent. I would spend four years alone as punishment for my foolish mistakes. But what had I even done? In the fog of my dream, I couldn't find an answer to that question.

Somewhere in the dark, I heard Mayi's laugh—shrill and sharp in the quiet night. I spun around to see a vision through the trees. A group of women—faceless fellow prisoners—tearing through my belongings, shoving each other, and fighting over my few, precious items. There, a boot under someone's arm as she yanked at its pair in the grasp

*of another woman. I looked down at my feet. They were bare. One by
one, the judge and guards began to vanish.*

"Wait!" I tried to shout, but no sound escaped.

*I tried to run toward the trees to where I had last seen my parents,
but I tripped and found myself face down in the dirt. I inhaled and
choked on mouthfuls of earth and burning cigarette ash. The moment
I began to push myself up and away from the earth, I suddenly found
myself thrown back down with force, a solid, crushing weight on my
back. Then, a boot on my cheek, pressing my face into the ground.*

*When the pressure released, I looked up to see the final two guards
retreating into the trees, ignoring my calls for help.*

For the second time in a single day, I was torn from sleep by the
sound of yelling. No, not yelling. Shrieking. I bolted upright,
drenched in a cold sweat, fearing another raid. The sound of Mayi's
laugh was still echoing in my ears.

The screaming was coming from the pregnant lady, of course.
She was shouting and banging at the cell door. Reorienting myself
through blurry eyes, I turned to find the laughing wasn't in my
dream at all. There was Mayi across the room, her laugh bouncing
off each of the four concrete walls, forming an odd, discordant
melody with the pregnant woman's screams. I half expected to find
it was me she was laughing at, but it turned out to be that she was
just in conversation with one of the other women.

Sitting up fully, I took my head in my hands, closed my eyes,
and attempted to steady my breathing.

I couldn't have been more relieved to find myself back in this
cell with all of these broken women. Though, I feared, I was breaking too.

Five more days.

THURSDAY, MARCH 4ᵀᴴ

HANNA

From Hanna's Journal
   More dreams. My jaw is sore from grinding my teeth. Never a dull
day but definitely our share of dull moments. The air, the mood . . .
everything is stagnant. Standing still.
   Then again, how a day starts in here is not always how it ends . . .

———

They may as well have replaced our heavy cell door with a revolving
one that Thursday afternoon. We had an influx of women unlike
anything I'd experienced so far, and some of them left as quickly
as they'd arrived.

It's strange, the range of emotions we went through anytime
someone new arrived. Admittedly, I don't think any of us could
help feeling annoyed. When you're living in a room that size, calculating whether you can afford to share a single slice of apple or
wondering how much more cigarette smoke your lungs can handle, every resource—square inches of floor space and fresh air included—is precious. Every time a new body enters the mix, your

mind can't help but recalculate. *Some for you means less for me.* Of course, no one wants to think that way, but that's just human nature, isn't it? So, that annoyance quickly gives way to guilt. No one *wanted* to be in that cell, after all.

That day, I felt a spark of stimulation as well. Within the first round of new arrivals, there were two women who spoke English. I'd settled in so deeply since Inara had left, I'd nearly forgotten what it felt like to speak and let the words just flow. We exchanged our stories, and I was once again unsurprised to hear these other women had essentially done nothing wrong. Nothing to justify being dumped in a place like that, at least.

"I've heard about you, you know," one of the women said to me after I gave them a rundown of my situation. "You've been on the news."

She must have seen the way my eyes widened in horrified shock at this information because she quickly continued. "No, no photo, no name. Just that they'd arrested some American woman. *Big time* drug dealer apparently." She rolled her eyes.

The way she said "big time" somehow made me feel better, unbelievably. She clearly didn't buy it, and she assured me afterward that the local media was a joke.

Still, it made me uneasy.

In the afternoon, they threw in a Russian girl with fresh bruises filling in on both arms. She was disheveled and bewildered and didn't seem to have the slightest clue what she'd done to end up there. Her bottom lip quivered as she lingered by the door, shaking and waiting for answers we all knew weren't coming. I gathered she'd come straight from the airport after some sort of incident with airport security. It felt eerily like watching a playback of my arrival so many days earlier.

Welcome to Egypt.

TRACY

Our room at the resort looked out over the most striking turquoise water. Everything was so still, so quiet, the view could have easily been mistaken for a photo if not for the waves crashing along the shoreline.

The pools, restaurants, and beaches may have been empty, but our thoughts were not. Around midday, we sat down in front of that window overlooking the water for a call with Ahmed, Amir, and Uzair. It occurred to me that the little table at which we sat probably witnessed far more mimosa brunches and conversations about sightseeing plans and dinner reservations—maybe even leisurely attempts at newspaper crossword puzzles—than video calls with Egyptian lawyers and the weight of the reason we all were coming together.

"March 9," Jon said to me across the table after we'd hung up. The words hung in the air as we both considered all we'd learned on the call.

We'd been stressing the need to have the lab results back by the 10th for days now. *Where had we gotten the 10th?*

"We must have counted the days wrong. When Ahmed told us we had fifteen days to turn those results around, did we miscount by a day? We have noted the 10th numerous times. I am horrified!" I finally said out loud after turning it over in my mind so many times it was starting to make my head hurt.

The odds were already stacked against us with an average turn-around time of forty-five days. Now we'd lost one more.

"We can't get hung up on this," Jon responded firmly. I recognized the tone. It was his "we have to move on or we will lose our focus" voice. "Ahmed seems to think the chances of getting the results back that early—the 9th, the 10th, whichever day it is makes no difference—are very low. Hanna will be looking at another fifteen days in that case. We need to prepare for that. We need to prepare *Hanna* for that."

That had been the gist of the call. It wasn't a shocker, of course. It had always been a tall order, and we still had plan B in our pocket. Ahmed, it seemed, had a plan B of his own as well. Although it was unlikely we'd have the results by the court date, Ahmed stressed the importance of working every angle we could to speed them up. He needed the results—good or bad—in order to submit an appeal for Hanna's immediate release. As long as the lab results were outstanding, he could not appeal.

We were resolved to keep at the impossible task. At least we weren't alone. Our contact in the senator's office had emailed that day as well, updating us on their efforts to apply pressure to our cause. The State Department had finally confirmed their knowledge of Hanna's case and further explained that the embassy was aware. They did not, however, supply any official answers to questions from the senator's office.

As much as I wanted something more from the US Embassy in Cairo, we had to move on. I really wanted them to be outraged and jump into action. I wanted them to check on Hanna and make sure she was okay and getting everything she needed. I just wanted them to at least care about our daughter.

I thought back to the mistake I had made in Googling Egyptian jails and sitting there horrified at what I had found. I hoped and prayed this was not what our daughter was experiencing.

Unfortunately, there would be no more news from the embassy that day. I looked out the window where a cloudless blue sky and half a day in paradise awaited us. In Egypt, the moon hung over Hanna in her cell.

I didn't get much sleep that night.

HANNA

While the morning had been a bore and the afternoon had been
. . . eventful . . . the evening continued to show me just how much
could happen in a single day. The first words I scrawled in my journal as it finally came to a close were, "Wow, what a night."

The Russian girl was given about enough time in the cell to
scare the life out of her. Then, they yanked her back out as abruptly
as they'd tossed her in. Within hours of arriving in Egypt, she was
back on a plane to her homeland. I found myself wishing it had
been that way for me.

I'd fully taken advantage of my sudden ability to communicate
in my own language, and by the time the other two English speaking women were released that afternoon, my mouth was dry, and
my voice hoarse. I was glad to see them go—neither deserved to be
here—and grateful for the way the blessing of speech had turned
my day around.

I was just sitting down to write when the door flung open again.
I can't recall the words the woman threw at the guard as he slammed
and locked it in her face, only that they were English, and her accent was unmistakably Dutch. Realizing her demands were falling
on deaf ears, she turned around and faced the rest of us. Her accent
wasn't the only thing about her that was hard to miss—the look on
her face as she took in her surroundings was one of blatant disgust.

She singled me out almost immediately. I couldn't be sure
whether it was my hand half raised in a meek "hello" or maybe

just my blonde hair and fair skin that drew her over to me, but I was acutely aware of the other women watching our interaction. Something about the way the air shifted the moment she entered the cell didn't feel quite right.

On the surface, I was happy to have another woman to talk to after the others had come and gone so quickly earlier that day—especially someone from Holland, someone I shared some common ground with. But as she told me about herself, I couldn't help but grow more and more self-conscious of the way our interaction was on display—specifically, how she was putting us on display.

Her name was Marieke, and she *did not belong here*—as if the rest of us did? From Holland originally, she had been living in Egypt for ten years. She was married to an Egyptian man. She spoke not a single lick of Arabic. She kept rattling on about the horrific conditions of the cell. She was genuinely flabbergasted. And while I don't think any of us were eager to throw a "Home Sweet Home" mat by the door or hang a "Live Laugh Love" plaque above the rusted metal sink, the revulsion dripping from her tongue as she spoke felt unexpectedly offensive. As she went on—the close quarters, the stains on the floor, the *smell*—my eyes wandered uncomfortably around the room. I wished she'd lower her voice.

Strangely, she seemed more interested in discussing my case than her own. Her husband, it turned out, was a lawyer, and she was quick to offer his help.

"This type of corruption," she said, shooting another loathing look around the cell, "is exactly the kind of thing he fights. Give me your lawyer's number—I'll have him reach out."

"Yeah," I stammered. "Yeah, that would be great." Then, after a beat, I tried again to clear up my confusion. "What exactly are you here for?"

She seemed caught off guard, instantly replying, "What? I just want to help . . ."

"No," I corrected. Maybe I'd been too vague. "What did you *do*? Why were you *arrested*?"

"Oh." A short laugh and quick shake of her head. "Right, right." Her eyes drifted away from mine as she spoke. "It was really . . . nothing. I didn't do anything."

When she met my eyes again, she wore a matter-of-fact expression. She wasn't going to give me details.

"Right, yeah," I said hesitantly. "That's most of us in here."

It was silent for a moment. Awkwardly so. Then, her gaze landed on my notebook sitting beside me on the floor. In one swift movement, she scooped it up, along with my pen.

"Hey, what are you—" I started, reaching out instinctively after my belongings.

But she'd already flung the pages open. I felt suddenly and inexplicably stripped bare. Before I could snatch the book back, she'd removed the cap of the pen and had it poised deftly over a blank page.

"What is it then?" she asked, not looking up.

"What?" I responded, too confused to make sense of it.

She glanced up, pointedly making eye contact, eyebrows raised expectantly.

"The number?" she clarified. "For your lawyer."

FRIDAY, MARCH 5TH

HANNA

From Hanna's Journal

Marieke left, and I'm glad for her. She clearly cannot handle a place like this. Her energy only got more manic overnight—she had not expected to be here that long.

On her way out, she told me again she'd have her husband contact Ahmed, and I hope some good does come of it.

Mayi is convinced Marieke turned down her offer of food because she is Egyptian. She's walking around now, mimicking Marieke turning up her nose. It was certainly nice to have company, but I don't think Marieke realized how quickly a vibe can turn toxic in a place this small.

A bad attitude is poisonous gas in a room with no windows.

She's gone now, and that's that.

The collective mood of the cell improved dramatically with Marieke's departure. When they finally came for her, it was as if all the negativity and chaotic energy she'd brought in with her followed her right out the door. A tornado disappearing sound-lessly into the clouds after wreaking havoc on a small-town street.

It was strange. At face value, it would seem Marieke and I shared a lot in common. It would be easy to lump us together—privileged white women completely out of their elements. But when Marieke was gone, order was restored within our little com-munity. The other women did not see me as they saw her. For better or worse, I was one of them.

I think it was for the better.

JON

As the boat rocked against the rhythmic rolling of the waves, I looked out across the water, focusing on that steady, solid line in the distance.

It's easy to get swept up in the madness sometimes. To let the line blur between yourself and your situation. I'll say that is one thing we never fell prey to, even in all the turmoil of those trying, uncertain days. We remained focused on our goal. We kept our eyes on the horizon and rolled with the waves.

I was glad we'd come to Mexico.

SATURDAY, MARCH 6TH

TRACY

The finishing touches on the documentation of the supplements Hanna had been carrying, which I had started from my home office days earlier, came together in a resort hotel room in Mexico. It listed all the supplements we had seen and deciphered from the "tabloid" picture.

Hanna's former company had been phenomenal. They created pictures showing each of their products in great detail, including the official packaging and a close-up shot of the capsules it contained. We had done the same for the melatonin and created a thorough listing of all the ingredients for each product. I felt I had become an expert on supplements, including CBD probiotics, THC content or lack thereof.

I was pleased with the final document, but there was still an uneasiness . . . *Will it be enough?* In all my years of parenting, rarely had I felt pressure of this intensity. The pressure of knowing that my daughter's well-being—potentially her life—might rest on my ability to help.

The final pieces to fall into place had arrived the day before— official statements from both the Idaho State Board of Pharmacy and the State of Idaho Office of the Attorney General, each certifying that the products listed and photographed in my document were legal under Idaho state law. It felt overwhelming to see how connections were shaped between "people who knew people," all wanting to do good. An amazing generosity of spirit and desire to help and go above and beyond were revealed to us daily. This is what created the document I was now about to send to Ahmed.

When Ahmed had asked if we might be able to get someone of authority to verify that the product ingredients were legal in the state they were purchased in, I am sure he never imagined all the people that would step up to help. The feeling of gratitude filled me with warmth.

I took a deep breath when I pushed the send button. It had a sense of finality. It was now in Ahmed's hands, but I couldn't shake the weight I continued to feel. *Is it enough? Have I done enough to free my daughter?*

Across the table from me, Jon typed away. He'd been communicating with Ahmed and Taylor, prepping her for her trip to be with Hanna. Ahmed wanted to make sure Taylor was completely on board with following his lead during her visit. The last thing we needed was to attract unwanted attention.

We'd all agreed Taylor should give her sister a message, something to keep her spirits up and her resolve strong. Something to get her through any possible bad news to come at court, as it was looking more and more unlikely that we would get the lab results in time—especially since learning we had one less day than we'd thought. We'd been thinking of just what to say, and based on the look on my husband's face, I imagined he'd found the words. I picked up my phone and typed a message to my sister.

I'm so grateful for the way people are stepping in to help. It's absolutely heartwarming! What wonderful people we have in our state of Idaho that they responded so quickly and with their full support. As Jon put it, "our hearts are crying with gratitude."

I hit send, then sat for a moment, letting it all settle in. Plan A was still in the works; plan B was put in action. Now what? We needed to prepare Taylor for her trip, prepare Hanna—in whatever way we could—for court. Would we need a plan C? I didn't want to think of that now. Only time would tell.

My phone buzzed. A reply from my sister to my text but perhaps an answer to my current thoughts as well. My heart needed this reminder.

Prayers are continuing. God moves mountains.

Supplements displayed at airport customs identified and labeled by Tracy

HANNA

From Hanna's Journal
This morning, guards came and called Obaida and Merjan from the cell for court. Merjan is free; she left instantly.

Obaida returned in a terrible mood. Something deeply unsettling radiated off of her as she deliberately avoided making eye contact with the rest of us.

As the whispers began, I tried my best to translate the energy into an explanation.

Anger. Indignation. Heartache.

One word I recognized again and again amidst the speculative whispers while we gave Obaida her space—"hatif." *Phone.*

That damn phone. It was clear by then that someone had one. But who? And *how?* Apparently, Amir showing up with pizza had made the guards more suspicious. They seemed to think I had called him to get us food. So, that's what they'd been getting at all along.

At lunch, we all sat down together. With a more focused conversation, I was able to grasp more fully what was going on.

Before they'd returned Obaida to the cell, they'd questioned her, searched her. Again, they were looking for the phone. *This is getting ridiculous*, I thought. Clearly, they'd found nothing. And Obaida had nothing to tell them.

"And court?" I asked, suddenly worried that the rumors of the phone were starting to have real, dire consequences. "Your sentence?"

She only shook her head, waving the question away as if it were the furthest thing from her mind. No news yet again. She was to return to court in another fifteen days.

I swallowed a bite of apple, and it went down my throat like a jagged stone. I tried not to think about how that could be me on the 9th. Returned to the cell, forced to wait another fifteen days.

When I snapped myself out of that depressing train of thought, I saw tears glistening in Obaida's eyes. One woman patted her knee gently, a sign of reassurance. Another rubbed her back. I continued to decipher bits and pieces of conversation.

The search had been a strip search. While we sat here in the cell, waiting for good news, Obaida stood in a room down the hall, stripped of her clothes and her dignity, while twelve men watched on.

I wrapped up what remained of my apple, the only food I had left, and willed what I had eaten to stay down in my gut. I'd lost my appetite.

———

I'm not sure if it was the unrelenting thought of the offense that had been committed against Obaida or the ever-spreading layer of filth—grime, smoke, and sweat—on my skin, but that evening, I was dying to get clean. The desire for a hot, deep bath, to submerge myself in clear, clean water, was stronger than ever. I wondered if I'd go to a hotel when—if—I was released on the 9th. I tried to picture a tiled shower, a warm cascade of water as I rubbed myself down with a waterless wipe.

I still wanted a book so badly, and I'd even asked for a Quran. I wanted to learn more about the faith of the women around me.

But I was still waiting. Often, I found myself reading anything with writing on it out of boredom. I turned the package of detox wipes over in my hand.

Waterless wipes. Great for use at home, in the car, or even at the office!

I let out a small chuckle.

Naturally, they'd forgotten to add *jail.*

JON

Jon's message for Hanna, as told to Taylor before her trip to Aghasour:

Think of all our hikes together. Sometimes the markers are all screwed up and the way is long. Sometimes you set out for what you think will be a short trek, but the trail drags on with no end in sight—remember Toxaway Loop? Those last couple of miles are the hardest.

Don't let it deter you. This hike, like all others before it, will come to an end. And just as in Hawaii, when I carried your backpack when it grew too heavy, we're here to carry the weight now.

I love you very much, Hanna! Lean into your soul, my girl. Connect with your spirit—it doesn't matter where your body is. Our love for you is taking that weight off your back and lifting your wings. Have faith in God, and you can move mountains. Always look forward and focus on the end of the hike.

It is coming!

SUNDAY, MARCH 7TH

A letter from Hanna to Ahmed and Amir:

Ahmed and Amir,
    I received my Quran today! I am so grateful for it—thank you. It's the most beautiful book I've ever owned. I received it at the perfect time. I woke up feeling a slight panic attack coming on. I was dreaming a lot about court and my family, and I know my sister is arriving today. I know you are both showing her the Egyptian hospitality that first made me fall in love with this country. I've been having more highs and lows here, as always, but this afternoon was difficult. When my delivery came, I broke down in tears. Tears of pure gratitude. This is the third time God's timing is far from coincidence. I have a strong bond with Him here and have my arms open wide for all the signs He wants to deliver to me.
    Thank you for this, Amir. It's already providing me with a lot of solace and, as you said, peace.

The Arabic to English book is a game changer as well. It will clear up a lot of misunderstandings and failed sign language.

I just wanted to send this letter to you guys as a quick note of gratitude and to tell you both I am doing well. Please send my love to my parents and to all my friends. Thinking and loving on you all. Please continue praying and sending positive thoughts for the 9ᵗʰ. I hope I can send you all a message myself very soon.

All the love,

x Hanna

Thank you for the fresh fruit and veg and the water!

HANNA

From Hanna's Journal

I sent a letter out with one of the girls to Ahmed and Amir to thank them for the books. After she left, I sat down and read the Quran. I hope to read it with an open mind and an open heart, without prejudice or assumptions. As I told Ahmed and Amir, I want to show God I am open to all His messages and signs.

My sister is landing soon. I have two more days. It's hard to believe I've already been here for twelve.

I spent much of the day reading, trying to keep my mind off of the outside. Some days, that was harder than others. When one of the girls arrived back from court, I asked her about the flight schedule from Amsterdam—as luck would have it, she worked for a Dutch travel company—but she said she didn't think any direct flights were running. She'd likely arrive in an hour or so on a connection from Cairo.

I wondered about my delivery. Was Amir here in Aghasour? Was he staying somewhere nearby?

Marieke had delivered some snacks as well—sweets and things. I thought that was nice, but still, my mind raced more. My court date was fast approaching, and I had no idea what was going on in the outside world. Were Taylor and Amir and Ahmed all together?

Had Marieke's husband been in contact as she'd said he would be? Was there anything to know about the 9th?

I put my head down in the book and inhaled the stories of Moses and of Ibrahim.

All in God's timing. It's just a matter of time.

JON

As Taylor traveled from Amsterdam to Aghasour, Ahmed met with the Ministry of Justice, requesting, yet again, a fast track on the lab testing. There were only two days to go. To our relief, it seemed as though the wheels were finally moving. They agreed to speed up the lab analysis.

We also received a photo of the letter Hanna had written to Ahmed and Amir. It was good to see her in good spirits, though my heart ached at her mention of the 9th. I knew in my gut she was holding on to hope for release, and the time was now so close. I worried that the likely—almost inevitable—news that she would be staying longer than she'd hoped would be devastating.

I sent a private message to Taylor and Erik.

I can see from Hanna's letter she is, of course, putting her hope on the 9th. Please share my hiking story with her. We are here to carry her backpack. There will be an end to this journey. Just the mile markers are not so clear. But we know Hanna is strong. And together we are stronger!

Things seemed to be going in the right direction, but two days seemed both impossibly long and still not enough time to get everything in place. I switched back over to the group chat to find the conversation had continued since I'd read the letter.

Ahmed: I want to tell you something. I always work on criminal cases, and I'm not emotional in my job. But Hanna is an amazing person. I really want to do anything to get her free from this. As if she is one of my family. God will support her using us.

Tracy: You are family, Ahmed. You are a lifeline for our daughter, and we are so grateful. We can read how special you are to Hanna.

Ahmed: I'll fight for her. We need to pray for those lab results, and then we can move forward. It is just a matter of time.

MONDAY, MARCH 8TH

HANNA

From Hanna's Journal
I'm happy the day is almost here. I pray my parents are okay and not worrying too much about me. I pray the lab results come in and all the misunderstandings are cleared up. I pray whatever the outcome is that it results in freedom.
Freedom to leave Egypt.
I have a feeling these next thirteen hours are going to go very slow.

The day before court, the energy was low in the cell.

Obaida was not feeling well, and I think it made her bitter toward me as I sat counting the hours until court. Unprovoked, she sat down next to me while I was filing my nails. In our broken (but improving) way of communicating, she told me not to get my hopes up, that our cases were similar. Her tone was not a kind one. Her charges were for heroin; mine *weren't even real*. How could she think she could compare us like that?

I kept my head down, trying not to let the negativity in. I could not let it affect me. Not when I was so close. For a moment, I resented her for sending that energy my way.

Ahmed had said he would get me freedom. That was all I could focus on for now.

Time in the cell that day seemed to stretch and drag on in the most excruciating ways, like running in a nightmare. My mind anxiously flipped through everything I knew about my case, fighting to get ahead of things, while the reality was that there was little to be done but imagine the seconds passing by on an imaginary clock.

I wondered when I'd see Taylor, why I hadn't already. I wondered if I'd receive an update from Ahmed before the hearing or if I'd be walking in blind, unprepared for what the day would bring.

What is happening out there?

JON

I woke early that morning from a restless sleep. The clock was ticking down to Hanna's court hearing. Less than a day away. For all the days we'd spent waiting for this moment to finally arrive, it felt a bit like we were now in an uncontrolled tailspin heading into the big day. Taylor had arrived in Aghasour during the night, and she would meet with Ahmed soon. The lab results, as we'd expected, were still not in.

I picked up my phone to find a string of messages had come in via WhatsApp overnight. They were from an Egyptian number I did not recognize.

Hi,
I am marieke.
I live in Egypt, aghasour.

—This message was deleted—

I met her in the Prison,
Can you perhaps call me?
You cannot trust the hired lawyer for an inch.

What on earth is this? Who is this woman?

I felt the blood rush to my head. I read it again. Then again. I started to sweat. My temples began to thrum with a pressure so intense, I felt they might explode. For all the progress we'd made as a team in the recent days, this message instantly took me back to the heart-sinking feeling I experienced upon opening that message from Amir in those early days. *I think maybe we've made a mistake. I'm not so sure about this lawyer.*

The messages had not just been sent to me. Before I had time to fully process the situation, we heard from Taylor.

Some lady is texting me. She says she met Hanna in jail?

This woman, Marieke, even sent messages to my nephew in the Netherlands. By now, half the family had read the contents. My poor mother was terrified. And we were scrambling to figure out what they meant, what to do.

As we soon learned, Marieke was a Dutch woman. Her messages—written in Dutch to some, English to others—were all urgent and pleading in nature. We had no idea how she'd gotten ahold of our information at first. It turned out that Marieke had, in fact, been in contact with Hanna in the jail—and the way she'd done so was alarming to say the least.

Marieke was apparently married to an Egyptian lawyer. They had a running scheme of planting her in jail in order to obtain clients. Something about it, and the desperate way in which she was trying to make contact with our family, was intimidating and deeply concerning. It introduced a whole new layer of pressure to an already extremely tense and stressful day.

Here we were, so close to the goal. Hours to go before trial. And suddenly, we were receiving all these messages telling us our lawyer could not be trusted, that we needed to fire him and hire this other man. We were trying to keep Taylor's visit as inconspicuous as possible, and here was this woman who'd somehow discovered she was in Aghasour and was relentless in trying to meet up with her. She claimed to have letters from Hanna and seemed to be using them as bait to get Taylor to give in to a meeting.

Frankly, the whole situation was a huge distraction we didn't need. Especially to Taylor, who had just landed in Aghasour. We needed her calm and focused. This Marieke, whoever she was, threatened to throw the whole situation into a state of chaos.

Taylor handled it beautifully. It could have been easy for this to cause her unnecessary distress at a time when we'd already placed such a huge responsibility on her shoulders, but she remained steady. Turned out the woman had her wires crossed about when Hanna's hearing was and indicated she and her husband were eager to meet Taylor there. Taylor didn't correct her and got her to send over photos of Hanna's letters. We had to keep our focus on Hanna instead.

Give it to me. Give it to me, Jon. I flashed back to my experience in the backyard. The moment in my mind was as vivid as the day it had happened. The serene feeling washed over me again. I found myself calm.

HANNA

From Hanna's Journal
Big news—I have a phone!

———

While the first half of Monday had left me feeling restless, things had changed when I'd received the phone. Just holding it, I felt I had taken back the tiniest sliver of control I'd been stripped of so many days earlier in that room at the airport. It felt like a sign . . . things were starting to turn around.

If it was a sign, some sort of gift from God, His next gift was a bit of comic relief. Gripping the phone, I wasn't sure who to call first. My parents? I had so much to say to them. Amir to thank him for everything? Ahmed?

Turned out I wouldn't be making any calls. At least, not right away. The phone was dead. Tears flooded my eyes, but I found myself laughing in disbelief. *Of course, it was dead!* But for all the horrid memories of jail I will never be able to forget, what happened next will stand out as one that makes me smile.

A few of the girls took the phone, talking hurriedly amongst themselves. Before I knew it, they were unscrewing the lone lightbulb on the ceiling, pulling out wires, and connecting them to the phone's charging port. It actually worked.

I'm not sure I'll ever understand how, but the situation reminded me once again—these women were resourceful in ways I could never imagine, not out of boredom or some unconventional hobbies but because they *had* to be. I was humbled, and not for the first time since I'd arrived.

When I said this scene had felt like a gift, I meant it. I think it was meant to lift me up before I spoke to Ahmed. With the phone holding some charge, I finally was able to get a call through. I was on a sort of high from getting my hands on the phone and from how getting it to even work had played out, but Ahmed's call was sobering. We had to keep it short, and he was very matter of fact and to the point. He was less focused on preparing me for my hearing than he was on preparing me for its outcome.

It wasn't what I wanted to hear.

TRACY

I don't think this is a good idea.

That was the message Taylor had sent when there had been mention of somehow getting Hanna a mobile phone. Hanna had previously written to Taylor and told her the guards suspected someone in the cell was hiding a phone. They had been brutal in their search, and though they'd found nothing so far, they didn't seem to be giving up. Taylor was uneasy about getting Hanna into more trouble. I agreed.

But by the time Taylor had met with Ahmed, it seemed the plan had already been carried out. What was more, Taylor left her conversation with Ahmed nearly certain Hanna was facing another fifteen days in jail.

We'd done all we could to expedite the lab result—everyone had. But as Ahmed told Taylor, things just moved slower there. Plan A seemed to be dead in the water.

Though I'm well regarded as being an eternal optimist, and while I'd been preparing myself for this possible outcome for some time, the news still came to me as a devastating blow. It felt as though someone had put a knife through my heart. Yes, this was why we had been working so fervently on plan B, but the thing about backup plans is that you hope you never have to actually use them.

That night, we sent messages to Taylor to pass along to Hanna the next day. Messages of love and strength and courage. Ahmed said he'd talked to Hanna, tried to manage her expectations of the day so she wouldn't be blindsided by the verdict. Hanna needed to be strong. We all needed to be strong.

I lay awake in a hotel bed in Mexico, my mind in its own imagined prison, thinking of my daughter so far away, sitting in one that was very real. I pictured her preparing for her hearing, no doubt bleary eyed from a long, sleepless night. I envisioned Taylor passing along all the words I wished I could say in person.

In our separate corners of the world, our family steeled ourselves for one of the most trying days of our nightmare.

And all we could do was wait.

TUESDAY, MARCH 9TH

HANNA

From Hanna's Journal
I've come to peace with the fact that I won't be leaving. I can't prom-
ise there won't be tears, but I'm staying strong and will practice patience.
I can handle whatever the outcome is and focus on the gift it is
giving to me.

———

I didn't sleep the night before court; that wasn't a surprise. I was a
ball of nerves, and I'd spent too much of the previous days trying to
pass the time until my hearing with sleep. When they came for me,
I thought I might throw up, the anticipation of the day turning my
stomach into knots. But somehow, I held it together, trying to put
trust in God's process.

The holding cell at the court was full that day. The women
were piled in wall to wall. They were loud and dirty. My first instinct was to keep to myself, but I'd judged them too quickly. Soon,
they were making room, shuffling and offering me a place to sit on
the floor, which was so full I could hardly see a square inch of it.

Probably for the better—the place was filthy. One woman bought us all sandwiches, and I have to say, it was probably the most delicious thing I'd tasted in a very long time.

The tension hung thicker than it did in our cell back at the jail. Each of us was waiting to hear what fate had in store for us. As with the times before, there was so much waiting. A couple of hours went by. I prayed for patience, prayed for good news, and tried miserably to calm my nerves.

At last, Ahmed arrived. I was called over to speak to him through the tiny, barred window on the cell door.

"Your sister is here," he said, and my heart began to thrash wildly in my chest. "Shall I bring her down to you?" Frantically, I looked around the cell. All those poor women, the stench of our bodies crammed together in the heat mixing with cigarette smoke, scrawls of angry writing on the peeling cell walls, and tears flowing from eyes of grief-stricken women who did not expect to receive good news.

"No," I whispered, choking on the word.

"No?" Ahmed echoed. "You don't want to see her?"

I shook my head fervently. I could hardly believe what I was saying myself, but I knew it was right.

"No, she can't see this. She can't see me in this."

He was quiet for some time, perhaps expecting me to change my mind. I bit my bottom lip in an attempt to keep my eyes from spilling over and said nothing.

"Okay," he finally said. "Okay. I have to go back up now to be with Taylor and wait for our time. They will call you soon. You're okay?"

I nodded, teeth clenched firmly, a sick, metallic taste filling my mouth. My heart ached watching him walk away. It took immense self-control not to call him back, to say I had changed my mind.

I sat down. I could feel Taylor there. Her feet could bring her to me in a matter of strides. But it wasn't right. I needed to be patient. In the bustling chaos of the cell, I sat very still and gathered every ounce of strength I could muster. I wanted so desperately to remain calm and collected in front of my sister.

I've experienced few things like that walk from the holding cell to the court.

Don't cry. Don't cry. Don't cry.

It was a fool's errand.

When we entered the court, my eyes searched the room. Suddenly, there she was. My beautiful baby sister. All my iron resolve to keep it together turned to water, flooding all my senses and rushing out of my control completely. As they ushered me to the corner of the room, the corner reserved for inmates to wait, I began to fall apart. The moment I'd seen her, I'd *needed* her. Why weren't they taking me to her?

I began to sob deep, uncontrollable sobs.

"My sister! Why aren't you taking me to my sister!" I gulped, but even I had trouble deciphering my words through my tears. I found myself gasping for air, panic rising in my veins.

The guard who was escorting me stopped. He turned to face me, and his eyes were kind.

"It's okay," he soothed. "Calm down. What is it you need?"

Overwhelmed to be seen, to be heard, all I could do was point and shout, "My sister! My sister!"

I'll never forget the intensity of our embrace. At once, the whole world disappeared, and yet, somehow, I could feel the profound energy we were putting off—our sorrow and relief intertwined—and the effect it was having on everyone around us.

I wish I could remember every second of those minutes with Taylor. As soon as we untangled ourselves from each other, she began to talk. Rapidly. She wanted to bring me up to speed, fill in every gap, every unknown, all the tiny details I was missing while trapped behind those four cell walls. It was more than I had imagined. I tried to take it all in.

"Mom and Dad want you to know they love you so much. So much. They want you to stay strong, Hanna."

My heart sank. There was something about the fervor of her message, the concentration in her gaze, the way she held my eyes as she spoke.

"I'm not leaving today." It wasn't a question exactly. I'd known this going in, had already spoken to Ahmed about my chances. It wasn't until that moment that I realized just how much I'd been clinging to every crumb of hope left.

She gave me the tiniest, swiftest shake of her head in response.

"But you will soon," she said quickly. "Everyone is fighting for you."

We spoke longer, and I tried to soak it all in, remember every word, every message she passed on from my loved ones. We were in our own little world for a short time.

Eventually, Erik came over to say hello. I was once again overcome with gratitude at the support of all these wonderful people. What did I do to deserve to have them all in my corner?

It was only a matter of time before the guard came and asked them to step away. Ahmed and I were allowed to speak briefly. I hadn't been wrong about people watching my reunion with Taylor; Ahmed had noticed it too.

"Cry when the judge addresses you," he advised quietly, nodding reassuringly as he walked away.

I looked over at Taylor and was surprised to find no tears. I actually *tried* to summon them up. But they wouldn't come. I knew Taylor's whole purpose there was to give me strength to keep going. I'd never imagined it would work so well.

In the end, I was never addressed by the judge. Ahmed and his assistant spoke with him at length. Other officials presented their points. I really couldn't follow what was going on. It all happened so fast I that knew I wouldn't be getting a resolution. Not that day.

All those days I'd spent counting down to March 9 flashed before me like some sort of delirious slideshow as I was escorted from the courtroom. No goodbyes, no formality of any kind.

When they placed me back in the holding cell, I was in a state of numbness. Tired, full of dull disappointment, I let my mind go blank. Another girl asked to borrow my pen. Mindlessly, I handed it over.

I pulled a folded piece of paper from the waistband of my pants and began to read the letter Taylor had slipped to me what seemed like only moments and somehow ages ago already. The tears I'd searched for in the courtroom came then.

The guards came and pulled several of us from the cell for transport to the jail. Only when we were in the van did I think to ask the girl about my pen.

The blank, apologetic look she gave me cut the last string holding two halves of my heart together. She'd left it in the holding cell. I crumbled.

Back in the cell, it was hard to handle the questions, everyone's need to know what had happened. Once the tears had started in the van, I couldn't seem to make them stop.

All at once, I couldn't handle the feel of everyone's hands on me, their hushed voices in my ears urging me to stop crying. I stood up abruptly, shaking myself free from the tangle of concerned women.

"Sometimes," I shouted, the word getting stuck at the top of my throat. "Sometimes, it's okay to cry!" I stared at the shocked faces of my cellmates. "Just . . . just let me be!"

I stalked away to the quietest corner I could find, scattering a few women clearly a bit bewildered by my outburst. I slunk down against the wall and finished reading Taylor's letter.

Oh, dearest Hanna,
I don't even know where to start . . .

HANNA

From Hanna's Journal

Thinking over my conversation with Taylor, reading all of the thoughts and messages from our family she had poured into her letter, something my dad said really struck a chord . . .

"Your spirit will always be free, no matter where your body is."

———

It took some time to process Taylor's letter, and at some point, the tears stopped flowing. Taylor had practically written a book. She'd carefully broken down every angle of my case, cited all efforts being made on the outside. She'd passed on messages from our family and my closest friends. She'd shared details of her life in the past two weeks as if we were catching up over coffee. I read her words over and over and let them fill the gaping void in my chest where I was sure my heart should be.

After some time, I dared to look up and around the room at the women I'd snapped at earlier. I could see the pain in their eyes. Pain for me. The guilt settled in, and I felt embarrassed. Quietly, I rose from the corner and went to my spot.

After I'd changed into my pajamas, I lay down, closed my eyes, and took a long, deep breath. I asked God for forgiveness and assured Him I was okay with His plan, whatever it was. I just needed a moment to be sad. I felt a hand in my hair, stroking softly.

When I opened my eyes, Aaida was looking back at me, radiating sympathy.

"I'm sorry," I mouthed, but barely a sound came out.

She only shook her head and continued to run her fingers down the side of my head, soothing me into a deep, deep sleep, my heart heavy with sadness.

I'd only slept a couple of hours when I was urgently jostled awake.

"Hanna." Aaida was saying. "Hanna!"

Exhaustion tugged at every cell in my body as my mind fought into consciousness. As I came around, I realized the cell door was open. A guard stood, waiting impatiently.

"Hanna!" Aaida urged again, shaking my shoulder, pulling me upward.

I was being called out of the cell. But why?

Clumsily, I got to my feet and walked to the door. The guard escorted me down the hall. I was still in my pajamas, still so tired I couldn't process what might be happening.

We turned a corner, and I saw Ahmed. He was smiling.

"Hanna, I have good news," he said, and everything around me began to go hazy. "You took your freedom! You are free!"

Everything turned upside down. A piercing scream filled the air, leaving my ears ringing. The ground slid out from beneath me. I felt my knees hit the floor.

Free.

PART THREE

TAYLOR

Those days in Egypt were hell.

Leading up to the trip, I'd been up against exhaustion on a level I'd never before experienced in my life. Hours spent holding a phone to my ear in what felt like fruitless attempts to get anything done with the embassy. Hours more spent cursing that phone while it sat silent, not receiving a promised call back. The wasted effort of trying to control the situation, the uncertainty, the fear, the empathy, the heartache—it all contributed to a rising tension, physically and mentally. On top of it all, I still had to work, still had a *job* to do. I was desperately clinging to all the little pieces as they slipped and slid, threatening to break free from my grasp.

By the time we arrived in Egypt, I was running on fumes. Erik and I had crammed ourselves onto a full flight for the first leg of our trip—a two-and-a-half-hour ordeal complete with minuscule seats and screaming children—and spent every minute trying not to acknowledge the weight of my growing fear and anxiety over what was to come. During our layover in Istanbul, we silently hoped that our next flight would provide, at the very least, a little more room to breathe as we descended into the unknown of the week ahead. No luck. The next flight was just as miserable as the first.

In the airport, when we finally arrived, the chaos continued. As I endured the unpleasant scraping of the COVID swab and tried to block out the noise—taxi drivers, so-called "tour guides," and luggage valets, anyone and everyone trying to find a way to get their hands on some tourist money before someone else did—it was hard to imagine Hanna here, just weeks earlier, filled with excitement and anticipation. She'd had no idea what she was walking into. I guess I did, and it made it impossible to find any glimmer of optimism in the situation. In that moment, I just needed to get to the hotel. I needed a quiet space to clear my head. There, I could cry. There, I could fall apart in comfort at the very least.

The hotel didn't exactly live up to its five-star reviews. The décor was outdated, and the bathroom tiles were stained and dingy. There was a lingering smell of cigarette smoke, and when I threw myself down onto the hotel bed, I practically bounced right back to my feet. The mattress was hard and unforgiving.

I didn't sleep well that first night, though by then, I wasn't sure if I knew what a good night's sleep even felt like anymore. When I woke, I did so with that surreal feeling—the one of being unable to place your surroundings as your mind reorients itself to reality. When it all finally settled in, so did a feeling of dread, taking up residency in my chest, clenching my heart.

Though I'd woken early, when I reached for my phone first thing that morning, I discovered a long string of unread messages. Something had happened in the night.

My anxiety only built as I caught up on the details. Some woman claiming to have spent time with Hanna in the jail in Aghasour had been busy the night before while I'd slept. She'd sent messages to our family in the Netherlands, to my dad, and to me. The messages were urgent, pleading. We weren't to trust Ahmed. We needed to fire him immediately.

My head swirled. I was set to meet with Ahmed later that evening. This doubt was the last thing we needed. We were supposed to be finally moving forward, finally working toward some sort of end. I was in Egypt to provide a semblance of strength and reassurance to Hanna, not to fall apart myself. And here this woman, in a matter of hours, had our whole family—including cousins and our poor Oma—paralyzed with fear.

What might have easily complicated matters but instead provided a little clarity on the situation was the fact that the woman's husband was an Egyptian lawyer. Convenient. What was more, she'd done nothing wrong—in the eyes of Egyptian law, at least—to land herself in jail alongside Hanna. Her husband had planted her there. The motivation was now clear and, honestly, not a surprise. Money.

It sickened me. From the moment we'd stepped foot on Egyptian soil—truly, from the moment Hanna had—it seemed like everyone was clamoring for any small part in our family's tragic nightmare. Any small part, that is, that might be profitable. The way I'd felt all eyes on me since I'd arrived, it was crystal clear to me now. As soon as Hanna had walked off that plane, her blonde hair and self-assured smile punctuating her arrival, she had been out of her depth, swimming in unknown waters with a paper cut. And the sharks were circling.

I resented that woman almost immediately—for the confusion she was causing, for the threat she was posing to our carefully laid out plans. I had Dad, Uzair, Ahmed, everyone coaching me not to let her in my head, not to talk to her at all. I ignored several calls from her. Until I couldn't any longer.

"Hello," I said coldly into the phone, finally deciding to just answer it later that morning.

Immediately, she began to ramble, clearly caught off guard to finally get me on the line. She was sinking her claws in. Her desperation reeked of self-interest, not a genuine concern for my sister. It solidified my direction for dealing with her.

"You have letters from Hanna?" I asked, narrowing in on a tidbit she'd supplied in many of the texts she'd sent.

"Yes!" she responded eagerly. "You're in Aghasour. I can meet you and give them to you."

Now, I was caught off guard. She knew I was in Egypt. How did she know? What if she was watching me, following me? What if she was working with someone we thought we could trust? After a moment's pause, I shook off the idea, needing to stay focused on the path I'd decided to pursue.

"No, I can't meet today," I said. "Too busy."

"Then Wednesday," she responded quickly. "In court. My husband and I, we will come from Hanna's hearing. We can talk then."

I paused again. She had the court date wrong. Instinctively, I opened my mouth to correct her, then thought better of it. Let her show up a day late. This could work to our advantage, get her off our backs.

"Okay," I said at last. "Send photos of the letters now so we can be sure they're actually from Hanna."

"Yes, yes, of course!" she replied eagerly.

When I hung up, I held the phone in my hand, wondering if it could have possibly worked. Might I have successfully conned the conwoman?

A few buzzes later confirmed it. I had the letters.

They were, in fact, in Hanna's handwriting, and the way she spoke so highly of this lady—Marieke—disgusted me even more. Hanna had no clue what Marieke's intentions—or her husband's—actually were. The fact that she'd kept the truth veiled from my sister only confirmed my suspicions. Why the need to put on a ruse for the person you are supposedly trying to help if your intentions are pure?

That resolved it. We had the letters and a pretty good idea of what was going on. Could we be 100 percent certain? No. But having faith, trusting our gut, following the path unwinding before us had taken us this far. We need to stay the course.

Erik and I went to the meeting with Ahmed that night with the weight Marieke had added that morning at least somewhat behind us. Which was good because the meeting left me carrying about as much as I could handle.

Ahmed leveled our expectations for the next day. The lab results were not back, and the likelihood that they'd be back in the handful of hours we had until court was beyond improbable. We were looking at another fifteen-plus days of Hanna behind bars.

It wasn't a shock but more of a sobering confirmation. My job there was not to receive Hanna and offer her a familiar place to land when she was released but to provide any stability I could, to boost her mentally and encourage her to keep holding on.

In addition, I needed to break the news that not only was she to remain in jail longer than anyone had hoped, but she needed to put her guard up. Those bars were keeping her in, but they were not keeping the vultures out. It seemed an impossible task: to lift my sister's spirits while simultaneously delivering the blow that could break them. I didn't even know how much time I'd have with her, if any.

That night, when we returned to the hotel room, I sat down and wrote her a letter. A very long letter. If our time together wasn't enough, at least on paper I could pass myself off as the practical, "put together" sister everyone was counting on me to be.

Another restless night passed.

Tuesday morning arrived. The heavily anticipated March 9. It was the day I'd been gearing up for like a soldier going into battle, but I was close to breaking. Where I should have felt prepared, I felt lost and unsteady. I couldn't eat; I felt as though I couldn't even breathe. I knew I needed to press forward, but no part of me wanted to.

I may be the little sister, but I'm the strong one, the stoic one. Always have been. However, that doesn't erase the fact that sometimes, sometimes, the little sister needs her big sister.

I stood in front of the hotel mirror that morning, shaking arms braced on the bathroom counter, tired and bloodshot eyes fixed on my own reflection, and allowed myself just one aching moment of deep, fierce, frightening need. Then, I straightened up, swallowed my emotions as I always do, and watched as my tear-soaked cheeks turned to stone.

We left the hotel and headed to court.

After a white-knuckled ride with a taxi driver who somehow managed to keep one hand in a bag of sunflower seeds, the other on her phone, and none on the wheel, we finally arrived at the courthouse.

We were greeted by Ahmed and his junior lawyer, both clearly dressed in their finest suits for the day. Pleasantries and small talk weren't on the agenda. It was time to go.

Brave face on.

Ahmed and the junior lawyer led the way, and I should note that from the minute we arrived at court, there were power dynamics clearly and immediately at play. Ahmed wasn't just leading us; he was pointedly ahead of us. He was establishing his ownership over the situation, and it wasn't just for our benefit. All around us, people gawked and whispered. Lawyers, prisoners, court staff. We were a spectacle, fresh meat walking through a den of starving lions. But Ahmed was staking his claim. We were to talk to no one. We were to follow his lead explicitly.

Ahmed disappeared to meet with Hanna, and I tried to keep my focus on the peeling paint on the dirty walls instead of the scheming that seemed to be happening all around us. When Ahmed returned, it was with the news that Hanna didn't want to see me. Rather, she didn't want me to see her in whatever condition she was being held in. I looked around the court hall, taking in the bedlam of the crowd and general disrepair of the government building. It was hard to imagine worse, and I didn't want to.

We retreated from the building to wait at a café across the street. Erik and I sat outside at an old, wooden table, the cloth draped overhead as a type of shade offering a momentary escape from the blistering desert sun. Erik ordered coffees to be polite, knowing I wouldn't touch mine, while I gazed upon an odd sort of large cage in the center of the courtyard. It housed only a sad, lone tree, and at its base, a single, dirty feather fluttered slightly in a barely noticeable breeze. I lost track of time as I wondered about the missing bird.

Had she flown free or . . .

We waited for a long while. Finally, Ahmed arrived. He explained that we'd need to wait until Hanna's case was called up to go back to the courthouse, and that's when we could see her. He had no firm idea of when that would be. I watched him look back over his shoulder toward the courthouse. Then, he turned to us and began to hurriedly explain that we were about to meet a man who was very important to Hanna's case. I glanced behind him as he spoke and saw a man—much more casually dressed than Ahmed and Rasheed, the junior attorney—walking pointedly toward us. Quickly, Ahmed explained that the man was the secretary of the judge, and apparently, we were to express our gratitude to him. He abruptly cut off as the man arrived at our table.

Immediately, Ahmed started showering the man with praise and thanks for helping Hanna, and Erik and I automatically followed suit, not really knowing who this man was or what he was responsible for. The man was all business. He was carrying a piece of paper, and after brief introductions and our strange show of gratitude, he turned it toward me, asking me to identify some white pills in a photo.

"Melatonin," I answered after examining the photo and recognizing the characteristic white residue on the bag the pills were stored in. "Our mom made a document—that should be in it."

At my mention of the document, Ahmed pulled a folder from his briefcase, opened it up on the table, and began to hand the man sheet after sheet of paper. It was everything Mom had worked so hard, so carefully, to pull together. I saw her signed affidavit that she'd personally packed the pills and official statements from the State of Idaho Office of the Attorney General and Idaho State Board of Pharmacy. And, of course, all the detailed evidence linking Hanna's possessions in the photograph to the original packaging and product information.

The man examined everything silently, eyebrows furrowed in casual concentration. It was impossible to read his expression. Occasionally, he uttered a short, clipped phrase to Ahmed in Arabic, and Ahmed would respond quickly. He seemed to have his answers well-prepared.

When the man had turned the final page—a document stamped with the seal of the Idaho State Board of Pharmacy— back over to Ahmed, he stood and left just as abruptly as he'd arrived.

Our conversation with Ahmed turned to small talk, though my mind wasn't fully in it. I was growing tired of all this waiting. I wanted to see Hanna.

We must have sat at that café for a couple of hours in total. At some point, Ahmed's phone buzzed, and he stood, saying, "Okay. They are ready for us."

Of course, it wasn't as straightforward as that. Once we were back inside the court, after making our way down the chaotic corridor that spilled into a large, central room, there was still more waiting to do. After the casual discussion of careers and Ahmed's upcoming wedding at the café, he had returned to his serious show of professionalism. Yet every time he or Rasheed drifted more than a few feet away from Erik and me, people would close in, begin asking us questions. Where were we from? What were we at court for? Ahmed would swoop back in, sternly reminding us not to speak to anyone. I wouldn't have anyway.

Instead, I observed. It was all I could do to pass the time.

When you think of a courthouse, the idea conjures up a system of order, no one speaking out of turn, policies and strict guidelines to follow, a sort of government sterility. That place met none of those expectations. The place was crowded and hot. Men in suits stood in sharp contrast to people in threadbare clothing and women in headscarves. No one smiled. Everyone waited.

Across the open space from us was a hall I'd been watching intently. It seemed to me this was where the defendants were escorted in, arriving every few minutes, handcuffed and accompanied by a guard. I waited to see Hanna's face appear through the crowd. When it finally did, my heart leapt into my throat. Our eyes locked, and hers immediately filled with tears. I clenched my fists at my sides, fighting to hold back tears of my own. This is what I was here for—to be strong, to give Hanna strength.

The guard shuffled my sister to the corner of the room, behind a barricade dedicated to holding the defendants while they awaited their hearings. She was coming undone. As she yelled, "My sister! My sister!" I tried with everything I had to hold it together.

Finally, the guard with Hanna turned to the crowd in the room. Instinctively, I stepped forward, raising my hand. "It's me," I announced. "I'm her sister!"

In a moment, we were in each other's arms. That's when the tears came. Her hands were clutching my forehead to hers as our tears streamed down our cheeks.

"I'm sorry, I'm sorry," she sobbed. "I'm so sorry."

In our minutes together—maybe fifteen in total—I tried my best to steer the conversation, to keep things light and fulfill my purpose for coming. But mostly, I found I just listened to her. Listened to her while she unloaded all the horrible things she'd seen, everything she'd been through. I tried to update her on everything I knew, but in the end, I slipped her the letter I'd written the night before.

For all that waiting, our time together was merely a breath, a blink of an eye.

Ahmed joined Hanna, and Erik and I were made to return to the hall to wait while the lawyers—even those who had nothing to do with the case—piled into the court for Hanna's hearing. Everyone wanted a piece of my sister. Again, all that waiting we'd done was incongruous to the length of time given to the case. Ahmed and Rasheed reappeared no more than five, maybe ten, minutes later.

I desperately searched their faces for some sign of what had happened. They looked . . . happy? I couldn't read them for sure, and they were, of course, unable to talk with so many eager ears listening on. Instead, they briskly escorted us down the hall, out the main entrance, and back across the street to the café, where we took up the same table where we'd spent so many hours that day. Every nerve in my body was firing wildly in anticipation.

After we'd sat down, Ahmed looked around cautiously before speaking. His eyes met Rasheed's, and they nodded at each other, a quick confirmation that they were both thinking the same thing.

"What?" I demanded, no longer able to wait. I'd had my fill for the day. "What is it?"

"The judge asked for time to consider the case," he said at last.

I looked frantically between the two lawyers, who were once again nodding and grinning at each other across the table.

"What does that mean? That wasn't what we were expecting?"

"No," Ahmed replied. "Something has changed. I saw it in his eyes."

"It was your work," Rasheed said to Ahmed then, his voice full of admiration and praise. "The case you presented. All those documents."

Ahmed did look proud. In truth, he looked like a different man than the one who had, just the night before, told me that the news today would not be good. This man was pulsing with pride and optimism.

I felt sick with adrenaline. This turn was not what I had expected, not what I had prepared myself for in front of the bathroom mirror in the hotel that morning. This time, the waiting was practically unbearable. Mostly because I suddenly had no idea what we were waiting for. The dangling promise that it could somehow be better news than we'd hoped for was excruciating.

Ahmed's phone rang, and he stood from the table, answering it as he took a couple of quick strides away from us.

The call was brief. Too brief. But when he turned back to the three of us, all our breath held tight within our chests, his face wore the largest smile I'd seen on him yet.

Hanna was going to be released.

What followed next was like something out of a movie—and not something I'm ever likely to forget. After the initial shock of Ahmed's news settled in, or honestly, maybe before it fully had, he was back to all business. The court needed ten thousand Egyptian pounds immediately. Then, before they'd release Hanna, they needed another thirty thousand. I was too full of adrenaline to even ask questions. I didn't care why they needed it—I'd get it to them.

Immediately, Erik and I bolted from the café to find an ATM. Was this really happening? All I needed to do was get this money, and my sister would be free? Was this nightmare really close to being over?

When we located an ATM just down the block, my heart sank as we tried and failed to wake the screen. It was out of order. All the coaching I'd been giving myself since we'd arrived in Egypt, all of my personal reminders to remain collected and not draw attention to myself, went straight out the window. Before I knew it, I was running down the street, my eyes frantically darting here and there, desperately searching for another ATM as Erik chased after me. Finally, we found one, and my fingers shook as I stabbed at the buttons.

We rushed back to the café, sweat dripping from our foreheads and chests burning, out of breath. I saw Ahmed's face instantly melt with relief at the sight of us.

"I was worried," he said sternly as he filled two glasses with water from a carafe on the table.

"I'm fine." I shook my head and gulped down the water and watched Ahmed's eyebrows raise as I handed over the stack of cash. I realized then he hadn't been worried about sun exposure or heat. It finally occurred to me what I looked like, a white woman who'd apparently lost her wits, running about and asking people on the street where the closest ATM was, then heading back to the café holding a ridiculous amount of cash. A giant target—that's what.

Ahmed took the ten thousand Egyptian pounds to the court-house, and we left for our hotel, now with the task of returning later with triple the amount. After contacting our banks and in-creasing our daily withdrawal limits on all our cards, we left our room in search of more ATMs. Luckily, there was one on each side of our hotel lobby. We split up, knowing we'd be limited to about two thousand for each withdrawal. One by one, I fed cards into the machine, extracting two thousand pounds at a time, reusing cards until they were rejected.

Eventually, the ATM ran out of cash. I joined Erik and watched with bated breath as he successfully completed transaction after transaction. Unsurprisingly, this machine eventually cut us off as well. We returned to the room and laid out all the cash on our hotel bed.

We were still about eight thousand pounds short. With a single working card in hand, we left the room again in search of the next closest ATM. Erik stood behind me as I completed one withdrawal of two thousand pounds after another. Every green checkmark of approval on the screen left air whooshing from my lungs in relief. I didn't know what we'd do if this card got declined. Four transactions later, my trembling hands clutched the last of the money we needed.

We texted Ahmed to meet us at the hotel. We had the thirty thousand pounds.

Mere moments later, we sat and watched Ahmed and Rasheed diligently counting out the notes, talking between themselves as they discussed next steps. It felt like some seedy arrangement. I half expected a briefcase to pop open, revealing stacks of illegal substances, or recording equipment like we were part of some elaborate sting operation.

After they were done counting and sorting the money, Ahmed and Rasheed left.

Erik and I looked at the clock. It'd been about eight hours since we'd first left the hotel that morning.

I sat down on the stiff hotel bed and let out the deepest, most tremulous breath of my life.

Somehow, I managed to eat and drink while we waited for more news. When Ahmed and Rasheed returned to the hotel an hour or so later, they looked ecstatic. Ahmed had just given Hanna the news. Our family had been texted. There were celebratory messages pinging in constant succession. The four of us posed for a triumphant photo with the two lawyers grinning from ear to ear. Erik talked excitedly with Ahmed as they reveled over the day's events.

A delirious exhilaration hung in the air.

But I couldn't quite catch it. Something didn't feel right.

TRACY

On March 12, three days after the judge's shocking ruling to release Hanna on bail, Taylor returned home to Amsterdam. Without Hanna.

Though the night before the hearing had been as sleepless as the many before it, we were lucky to somewhat escape the torture of waiting that Taylor had to endure that day in Egypt. As the sun rose that morning, it brought with it the news that no one was expecting—the judge had ordered Hanna to be released on bail.

Even after seeing the messages on our phones, I couldn't believe it. Of course, there were a lot of details for us to catch up on. And the effect was a bit dizzying, like picking up a book you've been reading only to discover you've lost your place and have been reading three chapters ahead.

Our group chats were full of celebration. Across the world, Hanna's closest friends and family were discovering the news. Even those closest to the case in Egypt seemed ready to start popping the champagne.

Congratulations, everyone! We did it!

That was the message from Ahmed. I responded that the news was incredible. It was. I think we were all in a bit of shock.

But there was one person whose texts didn't carry the same celebratory enthusiasm as the others. Taylor. She was happy with the outcome—of course, she was—but I could read between the lines of her messages and could feel her reservations a world away.

She was holding back. Something was weighing on her. I knew she wouldn't be able to fully relax until Hanna was by her side, free from the handcuffs and the watchful eyes of guards. Free to sleep beside her sister in a private hotel room, not some crammed cinder block cell. Truly free, not simply waiting on some promise of freedom.

In truth, I was right there with Taylor. I was afraid to rejoice too early for fear it would fall through. I was holding my breath.

When we received the judge's written order, it was in Arabic and even difficult for our new contacts who knew the language to decipher. Farris, our recent kismet connection—the one with ties to both Egypt and the pharmaceutical world—had a friend of his, a retired judge in Egypt, interpret the order. This retired judge was very surprised at the contents, relaying that this type of ruling was rare. That was the first leveling of our excitement and expectations.

The judge had ordered for Hanna to be released on bail. That was the explanation for all the fees, why Taylor and Erik had had to scour the city to find the money so quickly. Taylor—who, while everyone else was reveling in the exhilaration of the day's court outcome, had been diligently following up with the Dutch Embassy and asking for clarification on next steps—confirmed that this was their understanding as well.

Wait, what? She still has to wait for trial? When will that be? My head was spinning.

Taylor passed on what she understood—that Hanna would be released that night, free to stay with her sister or go wherever she pleased until her next trial. Ahmed provided no further details, instead letting us know that he'd have Uzair explain it.

Despite the nagging feeling that things weren't going as smoothly as they seemed, it was hard not to share in the enthusiasm—particularly from Ahmed. He was positively elated. He raved about the proceedings that day in court, how everything had gone so well. He reiterated the importance of the documents I had pulled together. His messages had a note of finality to them. We had done it. Hanna was getting out. The nightmare was coming to a close.

But was it?

Jon and I walked the beach in Mexico, and as God blessed us with the beauty of a perfect sunset, we held onto the hope that when it rose again the next morning, all would be clear.

Taylor spent the majority of that evening pursuing the details with the Dutch Embassy—indeed, she was on the phone with them well past midnight. The plan now was for Hanna to be released the following day but only after being transported to the National Security Agency for an interview.

But the end is in sight, so we just need to hold our breath a bit longer.

Days later, as Taylor returned to Amsterdam, we were still holding our breath.

Those days were a rollercoaster of intense hope and gratitude countered by moments of utter confusion and disappointment. On the 10th, we learned that the process to release Hanna would, in fact, take three to five days. Jon pressed Ahmed for answers. Ahmed responded not to worry, insisting this was all normal in Egypt, and everything was going to plan.

But it seemed no one had a plan at all.

In all the turmoil, we were still receiving signs. Signs that we were on the right track. Signs that someone was still looking out for Hanna.

To our sheer disbelief, the lab results so many people had a hand in expediting came back on the 10th—the day we had been fiercely focused on for days until learning it was the 9th—now just one day too late for Hanna's hearing. The timing was nothing short of miraculous.

While the turnaround time on the results had been the fastest ever (literally), it turned out to be a blessing that they had not been delivered the day of court. Official results would have meant another court date, possibly weeks in the future, to review. Instead, the judge had ruled solely on the evidence we'd provided and on the assumption that the lab results would support our case. We thanked God for His divine timing, for the judge's astonishing ruling. With many things still up in the air, these blessings were helping us to find the silver lining.

The biggest blessing of all came on the 11th. Early that morning, we received a message from Ahmed. It was a phone number and instructions to call it at ten o'clock that night (Aghasour time). It was a number for Hanna. We still didn't understand exactly how this was being arranged, but with all the ups and downs of those days since the trial, we were more anxious than ever to speak to our daughter.

I tried to forget the unknown danger the phone presented. *What if she is caught? How might she be punished? Could it further complicate her case?* But we had to know how she was doing, how she was processing the ever-changing news.

We waited all morning and into the early afternoon. When the planned time arrived, Ahmed told us not to call. Not yet. The surreptitiousness of it all gave me an uneasy feeling. Then, the text came.

`Call her now. Immediately.`

For the first time since our nightmare began, we spoke directly to our daughter. We heard her voice. It was Hanna! Unmistakably Hanna.

My heart was nearly jumping out of my chest. I had so many questions, so many things to tell her, but more than that, I just wanted to hear her voice. She sounded good. Sounded strong. The call was emotional, but it was easy to find the gift in it.

We shared what little we knew. Admittedly, it was hard not to be vague, considering the information seemed to be changing by the day—by the hour even. But now was not the time to convey our growing concern. We had to be a strong front and remind her that many people were working hard to get this over with—and soon. I think it gave us all strength to hold on a little bit longer.

Ending the call was the hardest thing I could imagine doing in that moment. I wanted to reach through and pull her over the line. I wanted to hold her in my arms and never let go.

Jon and I celebrated our anniversary in Mexico on the 12th, as planned, and we held on to the promises we'd been given that day. Ahmed called—actually, in the middle of our anniversary dinner—to tell us that the paperwork had been completed. The whole ordeal would be over in two to three days max. As we raised our glasses that night, we once again had a renewed sense of hope.

The 13th passed with no news, no changes. We kept our faith in the process, but our lungs were running out of air.

The 14th brought the end of our trip and also, it seemed, the end of our patience with waiting. The final blow was news from Ahmed—urgent messages that we needed to put more pressure on the embassy. We'd been promised two to three days, and during that time, not a thing had moved. Everything had come to a grinding halt.

As we prepared to head home, we started making arrangements for our own efforts once again. Since the news of Hanna's impending release, we'd given ourselves over to the situation, trusting that a resolution was in our sight. But perhaps now was the time to act once more.

I emailed my contact in the senator's office, my mind already back in Idaho. The subject line: `Can we meet?`

In all the anxiety, I walked out to the beach early that morning for one more minute of quiet and tranquility before we plunged ourselves back into the fight. We had an early afternoon flight, and I still had to pack, but I needed air.

My heart was heavy with grief and uncertainty. But the soft coral sand beneath my toes as I walked along the water felt grounding. The sky was filled with color, showing the promise of the coming sunrise. The clouds gave brief glimpses of the sky. The ocean seemed calmer than usual.

As I walked, I talked with God, and I had this feeling of peace that was further underscored by the rising sun beaming through the clouds. To my surprise, I was having a breakthrough of my own, pushing through the despair that was clouding my mind, my whole body radiating with positivity. I felt suddenly soothed. Something deep within me said, *This will all be over soon.*

At that precise moment, Jon sent a photo. A screenshot. It seemed that while I was having my own moment of divine reassurance on the beach, Jon was taking solace in that day's Bible verse. The message was beyond coincidence.

`The Lord turn His face toward you and give you peace.`

I felt the fresh air on my face and suddenly felt reassured that it was okay to breathe. And there on the beach, for the first time in days, I did. I let my lungs fill and knew we didn't need to hold our breath.

We boarded the plane that day with a lot of unknowns. All those days, all those weeks, we'd been looking for a finish line, the end of the trail, something to aim for. So many times, that point in the distance turned out to be a mirage, nothing more than a glimmer of false hope. But I had been reminded that morning during my reflection, "As a mother comforts her child, so will I comfort you."

I thought back to the message Jon had sent to Hanna through Taylor. It was clear now that the message was for all of us. Maybe the mile markers kept changing, maybe we'd have news in hours, days . . . perhaps longer. But we needed to keep moving forward. It was all we could do.

HANNA

From Hanna's Journal
I'm still left here waiting. In any case, it's just a matter of time. I
am a blessed and happy soul.

———

Shock. Relief. Pure joy. Disbelief.

I can't think of how else to describe the news of my release. I came back to the cell, the door shut behind me, but my soul felt like I was already walking free. Waiting suddenly felt like nothing. I sat quietly in my spot, my mind savoring the idea of joining Taylor that night, of sleeping in a real bed, of calling my parents and hearing their voices.

I watched as two women returned from their own time in court. One came back with a sentence of three years; the other, with the pain of having to wait another fifteen days. I was not blind to the blessing I'd been given that day. I could have been either of those women, and instead, seemingly against all odds, my prayers had been answered.

I was removed from the cell again, and this time, I was out for hours. More discussion of next steps, more waiting. But this time, the waiting felt like a breeze. I was getting out.

I was getting out.

After about five hours, I was taken back to the cell and told to wait. My stuff had been dispersed while I was gone—everyone thought I wouldn't be coming back—but I didn't care. I managed to reclaim my spot, as it seemed I might be staying through the night, and I got my pillow and blanket back as well. I changed into my pajamas and settled in, staring up at the lone light hanging from the ceiling and imagining that it would be my last night pretending it was the moon. The next time the moon rose high in the sky, I would be there to see it.

For a while, I lay awake and wondered if tomorrow I'd be on a plane, deported to Amsterdam, or if I'd be seeing Egypt as a free woman, allowed to close out my time here with at least a taste of what had been originally planned. I drifted to sleep at some point, my mind focused on better times ahead.

———

I slept long but not well. My brain was perhaps too wired on the idea that this would be my last night in this place. When I awoke, it was strange. The night before had felt surreal. The promise of leaving had given everything around me a sense of impermanence. But then, I woke to discover more of the same unpredictable nature I'd come to know in the past weeks.

I sat up, groggy, and looked around to find more had joined us in the night. Not unusual. What *was* unusual was finding a newborn baby lying on the floor. In a sort of daze, I lifted it from the floor and cradled it in my arms. It was filthy and too little, even for a newborn. It bore the hallmarks of neglect and malnourishment. But then, it smiled up at me, and I couldn't help but smile back.

I have to get out of this crazy place.

The other women began asking about my release, and the poorly translated conversations turned toward my belongings. Who could take what? One of the women asked for the literal sweatshirt off my back. I tried not to let it bother me, to hold on to the connections I'd made. This place brought out the despair in people, and despair can make beautiful people look ugly. Besides, much of my stuff was already spoken for, already gone.

I didn't care. I wouldn't need it anymore, and it wasn't worth the drama to ask for it back. Rasheed came, and I gave him a list of things I would need if I'd be there longer than just another day.

"And if I'm not released today, I'll need dinner tonight. Could you bring me some?"

He looked sincere and nodded reassuringly. He said he'd try.

All afternoon, I waited in silence, wondering when someone would come for me. The police, unsurprisingly, shared no information, if they had any to begin with. As the hours passed, I began to wonder whether I was leaving and tried to tell myself to have patience. *I was free.* The case was over. I could wait while they sorted out the details. What was a few more days compared to a few more weeks—months even?

———

I slept more and woke up on Thursday. It was afternoon, and it had been two days since my trial. Ahmed called, and I spoke with him briefly. There was a chance I'd be leaving tomorrow. The optimism in his voice confused me, but I didn't want to press my luck or sound ungrateful in pushing it. Still, in my mind, I wondered— *why aren't I leaving today?*

Ahmed said he'd planned for me to speak to my parents that night, and for the rest of the day, it was all I could hold on to. Little things were beginning to irk me, to crawl under my skin and threaten to steer my positivity in a different direction. Mayi smacking her gum. The ladies talking loudly while chewing with their mouths open. I missed my old pen and cursed the poor quality of the new one. And in the back of my mind, a real, deep desire to sleep in a soft bed was turning from something to look forward to in the days to come to something more like an itch begging to be scratched.

A fight broke out in the cell. Women were yelling and taking swings at each other. Screams of pain sliced through the thick air as punches landed. It should have shocked me, but by now, nothing did. I watched it all with a sense of removed numbness.

I am free. I am free. It is only a matter of time. I am free.

Speaking to my parents put me back in the right frame of mind and gave me something to look forward to: being with them again. They reminded me not to focus on a set time frame. Confusion was still coming at us from all angles, it seemed. According to them, it currently looked like I'd be out in two to three days. Again, this conflicted with thinking I'd be walking out any moment since the news on the 9th and even with Ahmed's most recent news that it would be tomorrow. But somehow, this didn't get me down. Hearing their voices made it real. It was so close!

After the call, I had beautiful daydreams to block out everything else happening around me. Hikes with my dad. Doing yoga or snuggling up for a movie with Mom. I knew one thing for sure—I'd make the most of every second at home. I couldn't wait to put this all behind me.

———

After the call with my parents, I slept through the majority of another day. I kept recording everything in my journal—I was a little afraid I'd start to lose track of time if I didn't. It was now the 12th. Friday. I tried not to start a mental countdown, but *Monday, Monday, Monday* kept ringing in the back of my mind. I needed to make it until Monday.

I was startled awake from a nap at one point and told to come out of the cell. Feeling awkward in my pajamas, I pulled my jacket around me and went with the guards. They were releasing my belongings (my baggage that had been confiscated so many days ago now) and asked me to check through it.

I'd taken my contacts out earlier, as my eyes were sore and scratchy, so it was hard to see. But it was clear things were missing. Since they'd been stored in the captain's office, people who'd been detained there over the last weeks had emptied my bags, using my clothes to sleep on. When the guards retrieved the items, everything was dirty. I felt violated all over again, but I hardly cared enough to truly be upset.

Just let it be done.

Back in the cell, I set my sights on Amsterdam. What would I do when I got back? I resolved to get a hotel room, to finally have some peace and quiet in a space that could be just mine. Even for a few days. The presence of all the other women—and now young children and babies—was closing in on me in a way it hadn't before. I needed space.

I spoke to Ahmed, and he confirmed the release would likely be Monday. *What happened to being released today?* I thought but didn't say. It seemed useless, and Ahmed seemed certain now. Monday. The paperwork was done. Only a few boxes left to check.

Shouting from the men's block in the evening caused quite a stir. When I discovered why, my heart sank. Someone had COVID. It wasn't something, even for all our bad luck, we'd encountered all this time I'd been in jail. What would it mean for my PCR test? I *couldn't* get COVID. Not now.

Just when I felt the anxiety taking hold, some of the other women invited me to join them in prayer. As the words settled in, I closed my eyes and once again let the anxiety make room for patience. I wasn't sure how long it would last once the prayer ended, but as if on cue, a beautiful serenade filtered down the hall from the men's block. After sleeping so much of the day, I knew I was too awake to force sleep to come, so I just lay down and listened. I'd hold on to the sliver of patience I had left and just wait for sleep to come on its own.

I'd be glad to sleep away every minute of whatever time I had left in that place.

———

On Saturday, I was awoken with urgency. *Get dressed. Gather your things.*

Hands shaking—a combination of nerves and hunger—I hurriedly did as I was told while the guards waited impatiently. *Is this it? Am I getting out for good?*

Then, as suddenly as they'd arrived, they left. Without me.

The confusion and disappointment only added to my exhaustion. Defeated, I lay back down to sleep. When I awoke, I was painfully aware of every cell in my body shouting at me—my stiff back and neck from sleeping all those nights on the floor, my dry and cracked skin, even the hairs on the inside of my nose burning from the cigarette smoke. My body was done, was drawing a line. Enough now.

To add salt to the wound, Sabura, a woman with serious mental issues, was back. She was frequently dropped in here instead of some sort of institution where she could actually be helped. Though I think deep down my empathy for her was great, her presence was bad for the cell. She spouted obscenities day and night and would remove her clothing for no reason at all. At night, she spoke in hisses and shouts. It made me feel as though evil sat in the cell with us.

Obaida left at one point, returning visibly disturbed. She was in one of her moods, likely having received news she didn't want to hear, and she took it out on me. She said she'd spoken to Ahmed, that everyone was lying to me. I wouldn't be leaving tomorrow or the next day. Three more at least. Anger radiated from her, and I tried not to take it to heart. I was on day two of the "two to three days" my parents had said. Ahmed was certain about Monday, which would be day four. I didn't know who to believe. The numbers were making my head spin.

Another fight broke out. This time, it seemed some of the ladies had had enough of the crazy woman. Hearing the commotion, the captain came down—a bad sign of things to come that he'd come down himself rather than sending a guard.

In a few quick moments, it was all over. He'd thrown Sabura to the ground, then kicked her repeatedly with such force that the whole cell went quiet from shock. He spat in her face and slapped her repeatedly until she too let out nothing more than a whimper.

I watched on, frozen from disbelief, all my own fight gone.

I need to get out of here. God, get me out of here.

———————

No sleep that night. Sabura's shouting continued all through the night, leaving no opportunity for rest.

I was borderline despondent with exhaustion when they pulled me from the cell yet again. This time, they asked me a handful of questions but gave no reason, provided no updates.

As they took me back to the cell, I turned and asked the guard, "Has my food arrived?"

A blank stare was all I received in response.

"Ahmed said he'd arrange for food. And water."

Silence. I was returned to the cell.

No one was sharing food with me. Hunger seemed to be a state I'd passed long ago. My stomach ached with a new level of hollowness I'd never known.

I was scared.

I was pulled from the cell a second time. This time, they took prints of both my hands and feet. They returned me to the cell, and I scrubbed the ink away, wondering if all this activity—even with no explanation given—was a good sign. Surely, they were prepping me to leave. I ignored the growing pain in my gut and reassured myself that I was just hours from release.

The third time they brought me out that same day, they transported me to a different unit—drug police, as far as I could tell—and I was asked to provide a full statement. They wanted a breakdown of everything that had happened. Somehow, it wasn't as nerve-racking as it seemed it should have been. These officers were more pleasant than most of the guards back at the station. I supplied the information they needed over the course of about two hours. I was certain now that release was coming. It was Sunday, March 14. Tomorrow, I'd be free.

As they prepared to take me back to the station, it crossed my mind to ask to just stay there. Couldn't I wait there for my PCR test? I realized I didn't care much about leaving all my things behind, about missing the opportunity to say goodbye to the other women. I just wanted to be done. I needed to be done.

In the end, I said nothing. I think I knew what the answer would be, and I couldn't handle any more external disappointment. On the way back to the station, I wondered whether my food had been delivered.

It hadn't. But I received a different sort of gift.

It turned out the drug police needed some contacts from me. Egyptian contacts, the friends and coworkers I had originally planned to meet when I arrived in Aghasour. They needed them to corroborate my story, to provide further testimony that I had not, in fact, been there to traffic drugs.

That's when, standing at the front desk of the station, a guard handed me my phone. The feel of it in my hands was unreal, and

I had a sudden, chest-clenching flashback to all those days earlier when I'd handed it over to the officer in the airport. My fingers trembled as I powered it on. Little red bubbles on my home screen indicated a massive number of missed messages and calls. I longed to open them, but multiple sets of eyes were on me. I navigated dutifully to my phone book to retrieve the requested numbers.

Just then, something drew the attention of one of the guards, and he stepped away. I was left alone with a guard I didn't know well, but I knew that I'd never feared him since I'd arrived. He'd made small talk on more than one occasion and seemed to possess a sense of empathy I believed the others lacked entirely.

Leaning in closer across the counter, he said in a low voice, "Perhaps you need an extra minute?"

I met his eyes and was about to tell him that no, I had found the numbers and was just finishing writing them down, when he spoke again.

"There's time. To find what you need to find."

Gratitude filled me.

I didn't know how long I'd have, and as tempting as it was to read all those messages waiting for me, I knew I'd have the opportunity soon. Instead, I composed a message of my own.

I typed feverishly, not knowing exactly what to say. I hit "send" over and over again, unaware of which message would be the last I'd be able to get out.

The guard behind the counter cleared his throat, a subtle cough, and I deleted the chat and powered down the phone. I handed it back across the counter as the other guard returned, along with the paper on which I had written my friends' numbers.

As I was escorted back to the cell, I reminded myself that this was all coming to an end. No more rushed texts or secret phone calls. I was certain.

Where is my food?

Ahmed assured me Monday that he hadn't forgotten me, that it was just proving difficult to send deliveries since the case had officially been dropped even though, unofficially, I was still behind bars. *And when might I be officially released?* I thought but didn't say. The fact that it was Monday and Ahmed was talking about getting me supplies gave me a queasy feeling.

So, there was no word on my impending release.

I sat still for much of the day. I didn't have the calories to burn. I stared at the wall and waited. For food or release? I wasn't sure which I needed more.

Ahmed called again, and I anxiously grabbed at the phone. *Please tell me you're on your way. Please tell me I'm leaving.*

He said he'd spoken to Inara, and she had dropped off a delivery of food for me. Had I received it?

No, I had not.

I ended the call, hitting a new low. I no longer wished to see any part of Egypt. I just wanted them to call my name and drive me straight to the airport.

Please, God. Please just send me home.

I'd reached my breaking point.

Tuesday, I told Obaida that if Ahmed called, I didn't want to speak to him. I couldn't hear any more false promises.

More sitting still, more conserving calories. Meager bits of stale bread and the overprocessed feta I'd come to hate were all that was getting me through.

In my stillness, I thought of my dad's words. My body may be locked up, but my mind and spirit were not.

Focus, Hanna. You are not going to die in here.

One of the women was taken out for her COVID test and did not return for several hours. They were testing her before moving her from the jail to prison, and I couldn't help but wonder—what if she had tested positive? What if *I* got COVID? It was certainly possible, all of us crammed together like we were.

When she returned, it was to gather her things. Her test had come back negative. I was happy for her and happy for myself. I assumed it meant I was likely still COVID-free. I was sad to see her leave for prison though, and I prayed that she would at least be going to better conditions. I was convinced nothing could be as bad as this hell.

It was clear I wasn't leaving today, but I gave her many of my belongings anyway. She needed them far more than I did. At least the end to my nightmare was close, as hazy as it was. Not to mention, I'd rather see them go to her than watch them be picked over by the vultures while I had little energy left to fight.

I slept terribly without my blanket and tossed in my sleep, dreaming about my feet stepping on Dutch soil. When I awoke, the woman lying next to me offered to share her own covers. I gratefully accepted.

Food was shared with me that night, though I sensed that it was a bit begrudgingly. I didn't care; I needed it. A girl who'd arrived and spoke a little English asked about my release. If I knew anything more. I didn't, of course. But she continued to ask questions. Would I be blacklisted? Likely. Might I get a few days to explore after they let me out before they deported me? I didn't know. And I didn't care.

I was done with Egypt.

———

Wednesday (was it Wednesday?) held more promises for fresh fruit, for vegetables, for water.

Ahmed called again. Again, he told me the time frame was looking like two to four days.

I supposed that meant four.

I despise this country.

On the 18th, Sabura was back yet again. Just my luck. The more time I spent in such close proximity to the growing insanity and negativity of the cell, the more my own mind threatened to release its grip on reality altogether. *What is time anymore? What is this place?*

Babies cried. Yes, multiple babies now. The other women screamed at each other all day long. I could sense a growing resentment toward me and all the empty promises of food and freedom, as if the extension of my stay was more of a burden on the rest of them than it was on me. They started to request payment for anything shared. I suppose they figured my opportunities for repaying their favors were growing slim.

Fine, take my money. I looked to Obaida, who was still holding my cash since Inara's departure. She gravely shook her head, a coolness to the gesture I didn't like.

How could my money be gone? That was impossible!

Everything is so messed up; how did it get this way? I don't want to starve in here.

I'm done.

JON

The day we traveled from Cancun back to Idaho, I was anxious to land. I needed to get my feet back on the ground and get my bearings on where we were with bringing Hanna home. Everything felt stop and go. Promises were made. Our hopes would soar only to then hang in the air and slowly deflate as the hours passed by with no progress, only silence. Ahmed's call during our anniversary dinner left us with such relief. Two to three more days max he had told us.

But the morning of our flight, his messages had a different tone.

Please, you have to put stress on the embassy to make the procedure faster, faster.

Ahmed now sounded less sure, almost desperate. Nothing was moving.

I knew we'd overcome most of the challenges we'd come up against so far by staying the course, trusting the process, but when we'd left our home for Mexico earlier that month, I don't think I'd really considered that we'd still be in this same situation by the day we came home. I needed to lay everything out in front of me, to look at the path ahead and make sure we were still on the right track. I needed to carefully consider all the tools, all the resources we'd be given along the way. Maybe now was the time to use something we'd been keeping in reserve.

At some point during our flight home, Tracy reached over and put her hand on top of mine. I looked over at her. Since that morning on the beach, Tracy had possessed a sort of stillness, a quietude that was reassuring.

Nodding slowly, as if to answer a question I hadn't spoken, she gave a slight smile and said, "Something is going to happen today. Something is coming."

"What do you mean?" I asked. "You think things are moving forward even with what Ahmed told us this morning?"

It wasn't a challenge. I genuinely wanted to know. I'd had my own moments throughout this journey. Moments that had left me feeling steady in my resolve. Moments that had left me sure we were not walking this path alone. Now, Tracy was there. I wanted to share in that feeling.

"Don't you think it has felt like every time we've hit a wall, every time we've found ourselves needing strength throughout this whole ordeal, it's been delivered just in time?" she explained.

I only nodded. She was right. After a moment, I said, "And then you had your moment on the beach this morning?"

"Yes, but it's more than that. Something else is happening. I just know it."

I hoped she was right.

When we landed, we stayed in our seats, knowing it'd be fruitless to stand and gather our things only to wait as everyone deplaned. We sat in silence, knowing we were hanging on to those last moments of vacation before we stepped into the chilly air of a late Idaho winter. We both took out our phones and powered them back on.

The first thing I saw was that there were missed messages. Not unexpected. The last weeks had been a constant stream of questions and updates. But during our flight, it seemed there'd been an unusual amount of activity. At a glance, the messages were from family. But one name on the list of messages received stood out. I felt Tracy's sharp intake of breath as we saw it at the same time.

Hanna!

While we'd been in the air, Hanna had sent several messages. She had her phone! My mind raced over everything that could mean as my eyes tried to take in all the words at once. It seemed the guards had let her use her phone while she was out of the jail making a statement to the drug department.

Her notes were short. I imagined her trying to get out as many as possible while she could. They were filled with love and gratitude—*I miss you* and *I can't wait to see you.* She'd been told she would be released the next day.

My heart was instantly lighter. It was so unexpected, such a surprise, that I was actually caught off guard by the feeling of happiness flooding my brain.

`My girl, my girl, I have no words. I am so happy.`

Her messages had come hours earlier, and I knew by then she might not have her phone. But I typed out a message in response. Tracy had been right after all. This had come just when I'd needed it most.

Gratitude followed me all the way home.

As with many times before over the last weeks, it turned out that those messages from Hanna would be another instance, as Tracy had described, of being provided with the strength we needed to keep going. When Monday the 15th came, we were hoping to wake up to another message: *At the airport! I'm on a plane!* Something to tell us it was all over.

Instead, our inboxes were empty.

`Ahmed, have you heard anything?`

The process, it was clear, was getting bogged down. It seemed possible that, in the local government's eyes, at least, Ahmed's job was done once the judge had given his release orders. Now, Ahmed was poking and prodding at a system that had no more use for him. They were trying to sort things out on their own, and any information given—to us, to Ahmed, to Taylor—was muddled, inconsistent, and full of false hope at every turn.

We spent the next several days trying to clear things up. Trying to just shake something loose. We fielded messages from family and friends as the news spread to everyone that Hanna was coming home. We didn't know what to tell them. Nothing seemed certain.

Tracy spent hours communicating with our senator's office, which, in turn, worked to get information from the Dutch Embassy. Messages were passed from offices in Cairo to offices in D.C. to offices in Idaho, and by the time the news reached us, none of it seemed promising. Things were moving forward but slowly.

PCR tests, likely five-year travel bans, the possibility of Hanna being tried in absentia and still receiving a sentence? Were these just distractions? We just wanted her out of there, and nothing was happening on that front. The embassy said they were "confident this will be resolved shortly." To us, there seemed to be no end in sight.

The days dragged on, and one rolled into the other. Every day that passed was another failed attempt to get anything done and another night my daughter was spending in jail. I found myself reading her texts from the 14th over again, siphoning what hope I could still find, knowing that she'd typed, *I should be released tomorrow*, and had since had to watch one tomorrow pass after another. *If I feel drained, what must she be feeling?* The thought was almost more than I could stand.

We tried—in vain—to advocate for Hanna to wait out her bail in a hotel. After all, the judge had ordered her to be released. Even all this distance away, I could feel Hanna's stamina waning. I was trying to carry her pack, but the trail was taking its toll. I wanted her out of that place! Anywhere would be better.

The idea was a non-starter. I couldn't understand why. She didn't have her passport; she had nowhere to go! She'd done nothing but cooperate every step of the way! How could she possibly be considered a flight risk?

It was an incredibly taxing, emotionally draining time. We were digging up every resource we had and using them. I once again reached out to my Egyptian colleague who'd helped us in the earlier days of the case. They seemed impossibly long ago by then. It pained me to break the news that things were not going as smoothly as we'd hoped. Could he do anything to loosen this log jam in the immigration office?

On the 17th, I sent a message to Ahmed. An uneasiness was growing in my gut with each passing hour. We *needed* to check on Hanna. I could feel it.

Can you please ask if we can speak to Hanna? This is so important for her well-being as well as for ours. If nothing else than out of basic humanity. Can he please just open his heart? Just give us five minutes.

I hit send and waited for a reply. When one didn't come, I added the only thing I could think of. The truth.

We are all suffering so much.

Another day came and went. It was March 19. Eleven days in total had passed since the judge's release order. And what were we waiting on? A simple fax ordering Hanna's official release and the delivery of Hanna's passport so she could finally leave. Two little pebbles jamming all the gears. Ahmed was calling on more personal connections. Taylor continued to have daily—sometimes, it felt like hourly—contact with the Dutch Embassy.

Then, we received a call. Our request to talk to Hanna had been granted. Another gift. Another much-needed breath of air.

Unfortunately, this call did not leave us with the same hope as the last. Our daughter, normally so full of light and infectious optimism, was fading into the dark.

"Mom, Dad . . ." Hanna's words were soft, her voice tremulous. The fatigue I could feel on the other end of the call surpassed any I'd ever witnessed from my girl. I imagined her collapsing in the middle of the trail, no longer able to put one foot in front of the other. The mile markers were lies. She was losing sight of the end.

We learned she wasn't receiving food. She'd lost most of her personal items. Her cash was somehow gone, though she couldn't account for where it went. The other women were telling her she'd never leave. She was dangerously close to believing them. The fear in her voice grounded me. We told her not to listen to those voices, that we were working relentlessly to get her out and that it *would* happen. But I could feel our words didn't quite land with her.

That afternoon, Tracy tackled our new priority. As she typed out a long, painful update on our call with Hanna to the rest of the team, explaining that we needed to get Hanna food and water, my thoughts stirred on something else. Something I'd placed on the back burner to simmer weeks ago now.

Plan C began to materialize in my mind.

FRIDAY, MARCH 19TH

TRACY

Friday was a long day, one of the most trying and painful of our journey. After updating the family on our call with Hanna and, as we were now accustomed to, following up on every lead, I sat down to think.

The exhaustion in Hanna's voice that day weighed heavily on me. Figuring out how to get her supplies—food and water at the very least—was, of course, the pressing priority. Her body surely couldn't take much more neglect, and what if she got sick? How would that affect the plan to get her on a plane? But as the softness, the devastating weakness, of her words earlier that day echoed in my mind, my heart ached with the need to get her something else: hope. How could we deliver the will to keep hanging on?

After looking over my inbox and the various threads of texts that pinged with constant communication hour after hour, I closed them all out and instead opened a blank document. My fingers hovered over the keyboard. Out of all the words swirling in my head, how could I reach in and pluck out just the right ones? Not knowing where they were leading me, I touched my fingertips to the keys and just began.

To our dear Hanna,

The range of emotions I have experienced over these last several weeks has been quite the trip. I have walked down memory lane from the time you were a newborn to just several months ago. In every memory, it was the radiant light you exude that shone bright. Through this time, I'm hanging on to the beautiful young lady you are and the endearing qualities of the love you give and bring to every situation. Your tender heart; your restless, wandering spirit; your infectious smile; your intelligence and curiosity; and your adventurous soul—all these things have been getting me through these long days.

Of course, I have also feared for you and what you are currently experiencing. My heart breaks to think of all you have endured. I have prayed vigorously for God to wrap His loving arms around you, to protect you and keep you safe, and to give you peace in the midst of turmoil. I have to remind myself—this is short term. I hope you know that too.

Our sole focus right now is to help get you out of there and then to help you put it behind you. Always know you'll find no judgment here—only unconditional love.

I just want to hold you.

As I typed, my thoughts flowing from my heart to the screen, I thought again of the purpose of my letter. It was a delivery for her soul. What could I give her to provide some sort of peace?

I know things are bleak. Maybe you can have this as your focus—envision all of us, your family, surrounding you, hugging you. Feel our warmth as we welcome you home. Make this the vision that you will live for, that will get you through. Picture everyone together with big smiles on their faces. Me and Dad and your brother and sisters. (Imagine how happy Kaya will be to have you home!) Think of us all in one great, big hug. Envision this. Hold on to it.

I looked out my office window into the dark of a late winter Idaho night. Tomorrow, it would be spring. I recalled myself sitting right here in another season, calling on God for the strength to make it through one of life's other trials.

I take comfort, Hanna, in the fact that you have found the power of prayer and that you have called on our loving God for strength. I have no doubt that this has helped you cope with this hard-to-imagine experience. I've been there myself. I, too, have given my grief and fear to God during the darkest of times, and it was in those moments that I truly understood the power of prayer. I know that right now, you may be losing hope. It is sometimes the hardest thing to do—to wait for God to show us what's next. But in the midst of all of this, just as I have before, I remind myself that God is never late. You have been planting seeds of hope with every prayer. Soon, God will send you a harvest. Keep faith, my love.

What else was there to say? I hoped with every cell in my body that soon, very soon, I'd be sharing these words with her with my own voice, holding her close to me as I spoke them. And there was so much to share. I wanted her to know it all—everything that was happening out here, not just *for* her but *because* of her.

I am amazed though how people have rallied behind you. Family, friends—even those who don't
know you—have all stepped up in big ways. All for
you! We have been so thankful for the generosity
we have seen. The supplements company gave us everything we needed in a matter of hours. The chief
of staff for our senator's office in D.C. has been
personally involved, even bringing on extra staff
to help coordinate information between the Dutch,
American, and Egyptian embassies. A friend in the
governor's office helped engage the Idaho State
Board of Pharmacy, and our attorney general himself called me immediately after returning home
from having surgery and hearing of our ordeal. You
matter!

Your friends did not hesitate to come to your
aid. They hired an incredible lawyer, and he joined
the fight as a stranger yet will be ending it as
family. Ahmed loves you and is fighting for you
vigorously. Amir has been so kind and generous,
saying you would have done the same for him. Lisa
has been checking in frequently, offering strength
every step of the way. Taylor and Erik—there are
no words that can convey my love and gratitude for
all they have done. And your dad—he is a rock and
an ardent sentinel that will do anything for you!
I want you to know you have a gold mine of love
that surrounds you.

I know that the help you've received has also been difficult to accept without causing you pain and guilt, and I realize that you have been doing a lot of reflection and self-evaluation these last several weeks. The best advice I can offer is to not dwell on what brought you to this dark time but to focus on what you are learning from it and look ahead to the tremendous opportunity of your future. Hanna, we all have things we need to work on. Don't let remorse consume you—look back long enough to learn and then look forward again. I know it can be overwhelming, often not knowing where to begin, but when you come home, you have a blank slate. Just start and build.

I wrote on and on. I wrote about self-care and the importance of loving yourself. I wrote about all her strengths and the foundation she already had to build upon. I shared quotes and Bible verses—anything that came to mind just to tide her spirit over. I wrote about how I knew that while she sat there in the darkness, praying for a light, she herself must have been a light to so many women around her in that cell. More than anything, I focused on love.

Hanna, I loved you yesterday, I love you today, and I will love you in all our tomorrows. I hope you take comfort and strength in this, as it is the greatest gift I have to give you. A mother's love is unconditional.

Love yourself, Hanna. Take time and see yourself through our eyes.

I will close with my favorite chapter. "Love is patient, love is kind . . ."

246

As I wrote out Paul's first letter to the Corinthians, I knew that was the greatest message I could pass on to her. All the details, everything we were doing, it all came down to our love for Hanna. All the help we'd received along the way, from friends and strangers alike—it all came from a place of love. Love for what is right and good. God's love for us shining through the selfless acts of others.

I love you to the core of my being. I want you to know there was no stone left unturned to get you out of this horrible circumstance! We will continue to support and fight for you until our last breath.

Love you always,

Mom

I sent the letter to Ahmed, hoping it would make it to Hanna in time to help salvage the last shreds of hope I knew she was clinging to. Then, I sat down with Jon at the kitchen table. It was time to take a closer look at our options. All of them. There were offers for help we hadn't yet acted on. We'd hoped we wouldn't need to, but now, time was running out. Every option needed careful consideration.

What I hadn't written in my letter to Hanna was that patience, while a necessary virtue, did not equal inaction. I hoped my last words to her conveyed the full weight of the sentiment behind them. *We love you, and we are coming for you.*

SATURDAY, MARCH 20TH

HANNA

From Hanna's Journal
    One month.
    When I departed Amsterdam on February 20, I could not have imagined what the next month would bring. I certainly didn't imagine spending it here.
    At least my dad makes a good point. We know this isn't forever.
    It can't be.

JON

I was ready to pull the trigger on plan C. There were reasons we hadn't, of course. While nothing we had been doing or dealing with in Hanna's case over the past weeks could be described as black and white, plan C fell in an entirely new shade of gray we hadn't yet encountered.

Through friends of friends and distant colleagues, we'd been blessed with many resources over the past month. So many people had stepped up in so many ways. But there was one card we hadn't immediately put into play. We knew that once we did, there would be no turning back.

The card in our back pocket had come in the form of an introduction a couple of weeks earlier. Yet again, it had come from someone who knew someone who knew somebody else, and eventually, we were talking with a man—apparently, *the* man—who could get things done. The type of things you needed done when the official channels weren't working.

Even at the time, the details were vague. Suffice it to say, if we called on this man to cut through the red tape that seemed to be holding us back, he and his friends wouldn't be bringing scissors. This was a last resort sort of option. If they weren't going to let Hanna out, someone was going to need to go in and *get her out*.

Even faced with the urgency of Hanna's circumstance all this time, plan C had seemed far too risky to act on. What if something went wrong? What if the situation turned ugly? We had to wait until we were sure, absolutely sure.

Saturday morning, I was dangerously close to sure.

TRACY

At 7:55 that morning, I looked down to see I'd just missed a call from Ahmed. I tried to call back immediately, but there was no answer. It was nearly an hour before a reply text came through.

My mobile battery is low. Don't contact anybody. I'm going to Aghasour today. Everything is perfect.

My heart faltered in my chest. *Everything is perfect?*

When Ahmed did call, the news was good indeed. When I'd missed his call before, he'd been sitting in the deputy attorney general's office. They wanted to tell me personally (apparently mistaking my elected official status in the US to be a bit higher than it was, but that is fine with me for the purpose that misunderstanding served) that the attorney general himself had interceded in the case. They'd be faxing Hanna's letter of release to the police station within the hour.

Through eyes blurred with tears, I watched as Jon danced—actually danced—around our bedroom and shouted, "Hallelujah!" Silent tears of joy streamed down my face.

It was hard to keep the news to ourselves but even harder to allow ourselves to believe it. We'd been waiting days for this very roadblock to be lifted, but we couldn't relax into the idea that things were finally happening. Seeing is believing, and what we needed to see was our daughter officially out from behind bars and on her way home.

I shared the basics of our good news with only my sister, not wanting to spread more false hope. Then, I opened up a different thread and typed out a message to the one I wanted to share the news with more than anyone else in the world.

We can finally breathe. We are so looking forward to hearing your voice again . . .

HANNA

From Hanna's Journal
    Just when I thought I was tired of journaling, I finally have some-thing noteworthy to write.
    I'M LEAVING!

SUNDAY, MARCH 21ˢᵀ

JON

Sunday, we woke to the news that Hanna had received her PCR test. Another box checked. Were things finally moving along? Apparently, with all the pressure coming now from every angle, the police station wanted her out nearly as much as we wanted her home!

First, the letter of release; then, the scheduling of the PCR test. Ahmed had also sent a screenshot of the ticket he'd purchased for Hanna. *A ticket!* We upgraded her to first class. She was finally getting out of that hell. I was elated, but the feeling seemed to be fused with an unavoidable nervous anticipation. It had to be real this time. It had to be.

The night before, Tracy and I had sat outside on the porch with our dinner. The air was crisp and cool, but it was officially spring. There was a change in the breeze. We'd toasted to the wheels finally turning, to our girl coming home. We'd speculated about what the final catalyst had been, and that speculation continued into Sunday as we sent updates to those we felt might have had a hand in this sudden progress.

Had it been the meeting with the deputy attorney general's office? Or the urgent cable sent from the Egyptian Embassy, along with the pressure from the Foreign Senate Relations Committee in D.C.? Or perhaps it had been my business connection in Egypt, Ibrahim?

Nothing was out of the realm of possibility. So many had shown up to help us in ways we honestly could never repay. But we would if we were called to, wouldn't we? Just as all these people—many of them little more than strangers, really—had for us. Wasn't that the point? I kept that in mind as I typed a message to Ibrahim.

Again, many thanks for the love and caring you have shown. I sure hope to meet you one day!

Jon

HANNA

From Hanna's Journal

  What a beautiful day! I haven't been sleeping, as my mind and body are preparing for departure. I almost feel refreshed. This burst of adrenaline is pushing me through these last moments.

  At Ahmed's advice, I haven't told most of the women that I am officially leaving. But I have told a few. I couldn't keep it all to myself.

  I'm just so excited!

I'd actually thought Sunday was my last day, but it turned out that my flight wasn't leaving until after midnight early Tuesday morning. It didn't matter. I was so thrilled that things finally seemed to be moving that it felt like nothing could bother me.

I'd been taken out in the afternoon for my PCR test. I was a little anxious about that. Every day, it seemed like more and more people were getting sick. I couldn't focus on it though.

I'm leaving. I'm leaving. I'm leaving. It is finally happening. It is.

My day was filled with silent prayers of thanks. I laughed when my food and water finally arrived. Rasheed apologized that it had taken so long. "We were focusing on your release," he said.

Better late than never.

When I returned to the cell after receiving my delivery, the sharp tones of bickering were ricocheting off the cinder block walls. It took me only a moment to figure out the cause. They were standing over my belongings. What was left of them, at least. Well, someone had spilled my good news after all.

"Hey!" I asserted loudly, but their voices only grew more strident. "Hey!" I shouted this time.

When the cacophony refused to die down, I suddenly found myself joining the noise, shouting louder and louder at everyone to stop. There was a bang of warning from the other side of the cell door, which, honestly, only added fuel to the fire. There seemed to be no clear sides; everyone was yelling at everyone.

Then, the door flung open, and two guards appeared. They were yelling themselves. Yelling at *us* to stop yelling at each other. The cell fell silent. The guards looked smugly around the room at all the flushed and frozen faces, then backed out, slamming the door behind them.

Despite myself, I found I was laughing. The chuckles rose up from somewhere deep inside my chest, and I tried to hold them in at first. But when I looked around, I could see I wasn't the only one who had seen the irony in the situation.

Now that the shouting had stopped, it was clear that tensions were just high. For over a month, I had shared this space—this ridiculous, cramped, rancid space—with these women. I'd seen countless faces come and go. I'd witnessed injustice, greed, unthinkable cruelty. But I'd also come face to face, so up close and personal, with humanity, tolerance, and compassion like I'd never witnessed before.

As I unstuck my feet from the cell floor, where they had frozen upon the guards' sudden entry, and made my way back to my spot, the crowd circling my things began to dissipate. And while I felt the disdainful sneers from a few like a hot brand on my back as they retreated to their corners, I reminded myself that they were not the problem. They were victims—captives—of a ludicrously broken and callous system, and I was about to break free of its chains. The reminder was humbling.

I'd like to say that those few women came out of their corners to join in the final dinner I shared with a handful of the women who seemed happy to celebrate my impending release, that we all came together in my final hours. But I couldn't begrudge them their resentment. Instead, I enjoyed the company of the others who did join in. We heated up potatoes and savored every bite as one of the women read aloud from the Quran. It was a beautiful experience.

As the words flowed to my ears, my thoughts turned to all the days and nights passed between those walls. It all flashed before my eyes. The good and the bad. The uplifting and the downright terrifying. The scariest month of my life.

I looked once more at the lone window of the cell and convinced myself that muddied shine that managed to break through was not the fluorescent glow of the jail's security lights but a sliver of moonlight. Tomorrow night, I'd be high in the sky, leaving all this behind me.

What a wild ride.

MONDAY, MARCH 22ND

TRACY

Please let the good news hold.

That was the prayer I was clinging to in the seconds before reaching for my phone—as I'd done reflexively every morning upon waking for over a month—after a brief bout of sleep Monday morning.

We were so close. And yet we'd been here weeks ago, hadn't we? Only to have our hopes crushed over and over. But each time, we'd trusted the process. Let them fill back up and buoy us a while longer.

But much like putting off a doctor's visit as if it'll spare you the reality of a diagnosis, waiting was futile. It actually hadn't been that long since I'd checked for messages. We had been texting with Ahmed as late—or early, I suppose—as nearly 4:30 a.m. Asking for any news on the PCR test results. Confirming over and over again that Hanna was, in fact, leaving Egypt in less than twenty-four hours. He assured us the test results were coming. Yes, she'd be on a plane just after midnight.

It had been only a few short hours since that exchange, and when I picked up my phone, there were no updates from Ahmed. There was, however, another message…

I know how to get her out.

It was from our Egyptian contact, the one who could carry out plan C. For the past few days, we had been exploring the option of plan C more seriously with our mutual acquaintance, the man who had put us in touch. Though no one wanted to address the potential need for it outright, everyone was starting to wrap their heads around the idea of plan C. But this was the first time the man had made direct contact. He was asking for an update on Hanna's case, and the last line of his message made my breath catch in my chest.

I flipped back to our thread with Ahmed. Still no news. Reaching across the bed, I put my hand on Jon's shoulder and woke him. I handed him my phone so he could read the message.

"Plan C would be ready to move forward then?" he said after a moment.

We let the idea hang in the air for a few beats before we both opened our mouths to speak at the same time.

We both hoped we wouldn't need it. After all, plan C came with significant and unknown risks. *Let's see what today brings. Trust the process.*

Nevertheless, I sent my sincere gratitude along with a summary of where we were with Hanna's case, all that had transpired since I'd last reached out.

I'm hoping you won't need to get involved. But we will let you know how today goes.

For what felt like the millionth time since this whole thing had started, I marveled at the number of people who had stepped into our fight. Through nothing short of the grace of God and the goodwill of men—of mere strangers—we had made all the right connections at all the right times. What were the chances that plan C would be ready to go *that* morning, that day of all days?

The message was loud and clear—we've got this. No matter what happened, Hanna *was* coming home. One way or another.

An update from our senator's office on their briefings from both the US and Dutch embassies reiterated much of what we had last heard from Ahmed. Though none of the news was actually news to us, it was reassuring nevertheless. Everything seemed to be in alignment. Things were moving forward. Still, I could have done without the waiting.

The morning passed at an excruciatingly glacial speed, but sometime around ten, we finally received word from Ahmed.

The PCR test was negative! Hanna was cleared to leave.

We finally felt that we could start delivering the news, that we had something real, something concrete, to share. It was nearly six-thirty in the evening in Aghasour, and Hanna's flight was set to depart just after midnight. In a few short hours, Hanna would be at the airport, and our torture would be over. The countdown was on.

Eyes brimming with grateful tears, I opened a message and addressed it to our family.

Hello, dear ones! I have absolutely fantastic news . . .

JON

The results of the PCR tests opened up a floodgate of emotions that would flow for the remainder of that day. I remember pumping my fist into the air upon reading the word "negative" in Ahmed's message and shouting—not for the first time in the whirlwind of the last couple of days—an exuberant, "Hallelujah!"

I'd found myself saying that word a lot. Nothing else quite captured it.

But along with the excitement of our pending triumph, our nerves were firing rapidly. I don't think I sat still for a moment that day. Like in the final moments of a big match, there were mere seconds left on the clock, and our team was ahead. But a single foot out of place, the ball unexpectedly switching sides at the wrong moment, and everything could change. I knew I wouldn't rest until Hanna was on that plane.

Our phones were buzzing nonstop. Messages were pouring in from family and friends—from Hanna's team—across the world. It was a time for celebration. In the back of my mind, I hoped it wasn't premature.

I received an email reply from my colleague, Ibrahim. In it, he confirmed that he'd checked in with his contacts. Everything looked good. Hanna would be leaving soon.

`Give it two to three days. Hopefully by the end of the week.`

But Hanna was leaving that night. She had a ticket for just after midnight, four in the afternoon our time. Wires must have gotten crossed somewhere on his end—I hoped.

The thought nagged at me throughout the afternoon. By all accounts, everything was on track. Then again, lack of transparency and misdirection had dominated the situation time and time again these past several days. Nothing would be certain until my daughter was on that plane.

I checked my watch. It was nearly three. In one hour, Hanna's plane would depart. *My God, please let Hanna be on it.*

TRACY

At 2:51 p.m., Idaho time, Jon was pacing our living room, typing with a focused intensity on his phone.

The entire day had been like this—grinning so widely that our cheeks were sore as we drank our morning coffees, only to find ourselves wearing a steady path across our hardwood floors as we tried to quell the rising tide of anxiety in our veins.

I knew Ahmed must have been busy, and our constant messages and calls were surely annoying him by now. Logically, I knew he'd respond as soon as he was able, but I couldn't help myself. I had to send just one more message. Maybe this would be the one that got a response.

Ahmed, any update? Are they pushing the limits one last time? Is she at the airport? Is she through security checks? Oh my gosh, why is everything so last minute . . .

I watched Jon move to the window and stare silently out at the clear day. I could practically see him doing the math in his head. She should have been checked in by now, should have been waiting at her gate. Ahmed knew that final payment was waiting on a photo—proof that Hanna had made it to the airport. That photo should have arrived an hour ago.

My phone continued to buzz in my hand, but the messages were from Taylor, not Ahmed. She was just as anxious as we were for an update. She sent emojis of stopwatches and praying hands, and we exchanged funny GIFs that illustrated our impatient unease. But outside of the chat, no one was laughing.

At 2:55 p.m., I tried calling Ahmed yet again. The line was busy.

JON

I keep seeing you typing and stopping.

The message was from Taylor.

I know. We are trying to contact Ahmed.

I considered my next message only for a moment. Part of me wanted to wait until there was definitely good news to share. But I knew Taylor was waiting just as anxiously as we were. With everything she had contributed to the fight, she didn't deserve to be kept in the dark.

We tried to call, but his phone was busy. Something has clearly happened that he is trying to resolve without involving us. Our patience continues to be tested. Just breathing calmly right now.

Our exchange was in our group chat, and Tracy typed back.

Yeah, I'm not breathing calmly.

It made me smile. We had a good team. I briefly reflected on all we'd been through, everything we'd managed to accomplish together and with God's guidance. This was just one more test, one more downed tree in the road. If it proved immovable, we'd just find another way around, just like we had every step of the way. It was out of our hands.

Still, the attempts we were making to keep the atmosphere and our attitudes light felt eerily similar to those first, early days when

Tracy and I had tiptoed around each sentence, not wanting to say the big, scary thing out loud. I thought back to February and our time at the cabin, the words we hadn't dared to vocalize—*we should have heard from Hanna by now.* The feeling was eerily the same, the whole situation was eerily the same, and it formed itself into a hard knot in my stomach.

It was 3:05 p.m. Still no news. The plane was now leaving in less than an hour. When my phone buzzed again, it was a screenshot from Taylor. It was a text exchange with Rasheed. Ahmed had insisted not to contact Rasheed that day as everything unfolded, but Taylor's anxiety must have gotten the best of her, and she'd messaged the junior lawyer directly for an update. His reply was short.

`It's okay. Wait for her at the airport at 11:00 p.m.`

When she texted back to confirm that Hanna was, in fact, at the airport and through security, there was no further response.

"Why aren't they telling us more?" I demanded aloud, speaking to no one in particular. I couldn't help but wonder what they were playing at. Was it all a giant ruse? Who could we really trust? Was this some sort of last-minute show of power?

It was 3:23 p.m. Nothing. By this point, it was surely impossible that she could make an international flight within half an hour.

At 3:26, a message from Ahmed appeared. It was a photo forwarded to him by Rasheed. I'm sure my heart stopped beating in my chest.

Hanna was at the airport! The photo showed Hanna sitting in a chair, holding on to an assortment of bags and luggage. What a beautiful picture! What an incredible picture! I had been dreaming of receiving that picture from the moment we'd had our first video call with Ahmed and negotiated the fees. And, at last, it had finally arrived. It was finally real.

Hallelujah!

Again, it was the first word that came to mind. The only word resounding in my heart. I could have screamed it from the top of my lungs.

But has she checked in? Is she through security? Even with the elation I felt, my mind considered the time. Her international flight was scheduled to depart in thirty minutes. The other passengers had likely started boarding. Time was running out . . .

HANNA

At airport security, I sat in a hard plastic chair, fumbling through my belongings, which were piled precariously on my lap and held between my feet on the floor. My hands shook as my fingers paused for a moment over the sturdy leather cover of my passport. I continued pushing around the various contents of my purse, frantically searching until I could be sure I had it—my phone. When my fingertips landed on the rigid case, I clutched it hard in my palm.

I knew these two items had been there on the drive to the airport, had confirmed it several times, but as I prepared to go through security and then head to my gate—to my plane—the whole scenario felt dreamlike and unreal. I had to be sure. It had been a month earlier in this very airport that my passport and phone had been ripped from me. In an instant, my freedom and all connection to everyone I loved—gone. Taken.

I took a breath, my grip loosening, and I dropped the phone back into the safety of my purse. This was really happening. I was really leaving.

At the unmistakable imitation shutter noise of a camera, I looked up to see Rasheed's phone aimed squarely at me.

"For your parents," he explained, and as an instinctual reaction, I forced an awkward smile for the camera. But before my smile was in place, Rasheed was already lowering the phone to type and send the one he'd taken without warning.

Proof, I thought. That's what he was sending. Proof that I'd made it to the airport, that I was on my way home. Not, as I'd mistakenly assumed, a celebratory snapshot of my freedom.

But I *was* free. I *was* on my way out of this place. That was what mattered.

Hours earlier—even just moments earlier, if I'm being honest—I wasn't sure I would ever make it out. True to the chaotic nature of how everything had played out over the last several weeks, the day of my departure didn't go as smoothly as I'd perhaps naively imagined it would. Every step of the process—waiting in the cell to be called out, my official release from the jail, signatures on endless sheets of paper, a meandering drive through seemingly endless traffic—seemed to drag on at a nightmarishly slow pace, all while the clock ticked steadily by and the hour of my flight's departure grew ominously closer. In the back of the car, as we hit yet another detour, another delay, I closed my eyes tight and prayed we'd make it.

And then, there I was with barely minutes to spare.

Once Rasheed had sent the photo, there was hardly time for formal goodbyes. In truth, I didn't know what to say anyway. As I uttered "thank you" to Rasheed, officers approached, hurriedly grabbing my belongings and cuffing my wrists. Panic bubbled up in my chest, and my voice caught in my throat. I could hardly manage the word, "Why?"

"We need to escort you to your plane. Come now. Your flight is departing."

While we rushed through the airport, I could feel the color rising in my cheeks as the eyes of dozens of strangers landed upon me. With a sharp pang, I realized that even through the fear, anger, and inhumanity of my stay in Egypt for the last month, I had been spared one discomfort. Surrounded by the women in the cell and others at court, I had never been faced with such a public display of my shame and humiliation. What were these people thinking I'd done? What crimes were they assigning to the disheveled and disoriented white girl being hurriedly pushed to her deportation? Would any of them afford me sympathy?

With my feet carrying me closer and closer to my gate and final calls for flights—*my flight?*—sounding over the speaker system, I had the overwhelming desire for this part to be over. I couldn't take the stares. I couldn't take the thought of missing the flight and sitting, handcuffed and branded a criminal for all the world to see, for hours until another flight could be secured. Or worse—taken back to the station and dumped right back into my nightmare.

But then we were at the gate. The seats all around were empty. The door to the jet bridge was closed.

TRACY AND JON

The minutes that passed after we received the photo of Hanna sitting at airport security were some of the longest, most nerve-racking of the entire ordeal. She had made it to the airport, yes. But her flight's departure was imminent. It seemed impossible that she would make it. And what then?

We tried not to think of the answer to that question. After weeks of navigating every roadblock, every bump, every detour, our minds and hearts had had enough of the "what thens" and "what ifs." Even as they coursed through our brains, we dared not wonder them aloud to each other.

We continued to wait and hope and trust. We sat unspeaking on the couch, silent prayers hanging heavy in the air of a quiet house. Did either of us breathe a single breath during those achingly long moments? We're still not sure.

Until the call came. The call we'd been waiting for all those minutes, hours, days, and weeks, through sleepless nights and prayer-fueled days. The call that let us know we could finally breathe again.

Seeing Hanna's name on the screen, we couldn't answer fast enough. When her beautiful face appeared, the nervous smile and glimmer of relief in her eyes told us everything we needed to know. And the tears. Tears of relief, of joy, and of the sorrow of the last thirty days leading up to this single moment. We could breathe again.

Our nightmare was over. She was on the plane.

HANNA

From Hanna's Journal
   Guys . . . I'm free!

———

I ended the FaceTime call with Mom and Dad, cheeks damp and eyes stinging. My dad's words were echoing in my mind and pounding in my heart.

"Hanna, cry. It's okay. Everything is okay."

And cry I did. Though if I'm honest, I'm not sure how I had any tears left by then. I'd spent thirty days crying. Crying tears born out of anguish, guilt, hope, fear. Now, all that was behind me, and there I was, sitting in business class on a plane that would soon take off and fly me right back to where my journey had begun weeks ago. And I was crying.

Was it relief? Disbelief? I didn't know. But it felt like release.

I was free.

It was all a bit surreal. For weeks, I had thought about everything I'd do—every call I'd make, every text I'd send—the very moment I was able. But now, I didn't know where to begin. I had apologies to make, so much gratitude to express.

And the women I'd left behind . . . my mind was already buzzing with the need to do something for them, to put my experience—and my privilege—to use in their favor. My pen was flying across the lines of the notebook splayed out on the tray table in front of me, a flurry of notes in its wake. I was making a record, jotting down everything that came to mind. The conditions. The ridiculous charges and even more outlandish sentences some of those women were facing. I wrote until my hand ached.

Reluctantly, I set the pen down. It'd be a long time before I forgot the details. Never, I suspected.

Taking in the other passengers of the plane, I wondered whether anyone was looking forward to sleeping in a bed more than I was. Not likely. For someone who'd done little else but sleep for thirty-two days, I was exhausted.

I closed the notebook, but instead of putting it away, I clutched it firmly in my lap. I relaxed against the seat—the first soft surface my body had touched in weeks—and closed my eyes. What I felt next took me by surprise. Not because it was unexpected—I'd felt the plane taxiing down the runway, had heard the messages from the flight attendants to prepare for takeoff—but because I realized in that moment that part of me thought it was something I would never experience again. That momentary feeling of weightlessness—the kind where your heart seems to float freely in your chest—as the wheels lifted from the ground and the plane took to the air. Just like that, I had left Egypt.

Thank you, God. Thank you.

When I opened my eyes again, I turned them toward the window beside me. I didn't look down at the country, the memories, the people, or the nightmare I was leaving behind. What I was searching for was right in front of me.

As the plane flew toward Istanbul in the dark hours of the morning and the miles grew between Egypt and me, the moon lit the way right beside me. All those nights, even when I couldn't see it with my own two eyes, it had been there all along, knowing one day it would guide me home.

EPILOGUE

"We know that in everything God works for the good
of those who love him. They are the people he called,
because that was his plan."
(Romans 8:28)

This is a true story. And because it is a true story, it doesn't end
neatly with Hanna on a plane, Egypt growing ever smaller in the
distance until it was nothing but a bad memory by the time her
plane touched down in Amsterdam. True, that day, it felt like the
nightmare was finally over, and in many ways, it was. For what
was likely the longest and most trying month of our lives, we had
fought toward our goal: bring Hanna home. If this were a movie,
that is where the story would have ended. But this is not a movie.

That night, and in the days immediately following Hanna's
triumphant release, we celebrated. Friends and family joined us in
our home, we cried tears of relief and joy, we broke out the champagne. It was probably the best champagne we'd had in our lives,
so sweet was our cause for celebration. When Hanna was finally
reunited with Taylor, they sent a photo of the two of them together
in Taylor's apartment, smiling as if everything was once again right
in the world. And for a moment, it was.

The reality of the situation is that what Hanna had been through—what we'd all been through—wasn't confined tidily within the marked calendar days of her imprisonment or tucked safely behind Egyptian borders. While we celebrated and thanked God for an end to our nightmare, it had never really been a nightmare. There was no waking up, no shrugging off residual terror that was simply a creation of our imaginations. For more than thirty days, we'd *lived* that nightmare. It will be a part of us—all of us—forever.

As parents, the predominant feelings in the days that followed Hanna's release were those of gratitude. We knew that there would be challenges ahead, and we had done much to prepare for them. Before Hanna had even stepped foot back in the Netherlands, Taylor had pulled information together for her as a resource guide. She had family and friends write notes and emails of support so that Hanna was embraced by the love of those who supported her and was showered with positive affirmations. We'd sourced counseling for her, arranged for medical evaluations.

Tracy immediately began making travel arrangements to finally go to her and hold her in her arms. But at the time, the world was still in the midst of the COVID-19 pandemic, and since travel to the Netherlands was not allowed for non-citizens, it would be many more months before we were together again. Still, the relief and thankfulness we felt at our daughter's physical safety was paramount.

Hanna's feelings in the aftermath of her ordeal were not as straightforward. The truth of it is that Hanna struggled. For her, freedom was laden with obstacles and implications. The trauma, fear, and pain were not suddenly wiped away the moment she boarded that plane as a free woman. Neither was her guilt. In the days and months that followed, Hanna grappled with the memories, the trauma, and the reality of what she'd lived through, all she'd witnessed and experienced firsthand. She still had court hearings that needed attention from afar. Though the judge had ordered

Hanna to be released from jail and allowed her to travel back to Amsterdam, the charges had not yet been officially dropped and still needed legal attention. Hers was a long road ahead, and in many ways, she will carry the weight of that month in Egypt with her for the rest of her life.

While it may not have been a choice for Hanna to live with the haunting memories of that time, if given the opportunity, many might have chosen to simply wash their hands of the experience and never look back. But that's not Hanna. In fact, Hanna was still in the air when she began writing in her journal again. No longer chronicling the horrendous circumstances and unspeakable injustices but instead planning her fight against them.

We know the tremendous effort and faith that went into Hanna's release. Yet it is not lost on any of us that Hanna's story could have—would have—ended much differently if it weren't for the connections we made, the resources we harnessed, and our unyielding resolve to fight until we had nothing left. We were humbled in our victory, but none more so than Hanna. She knew even sitting on that plane that while the echoes of her nightmare would visit her for many nights to come, she'd experience them with the support of friends and family while lying in a soft bed under clean blankets, surrounded by four walls of her choosing and a door that locked from the inside. How many of the women she'd met in that jail would ever know that privilege?

And so, no sooner had Hanna tasted freedom than she began plotting how she could apply all that guilt, all that anguish over the seemingly random advantages she'd been afforded in life, and use it to help. After her release, Hanna was able to lend financial and legal assistance that would lead to the release of two of Hanna's cellmates whom she had deeply connected with.

Again, this is not a movie. If the entire system could have been reformed on sheer passion and strength of will alone, Hanna would have taken it down in a single day. Instead, this is the real world, and three women walking free is nothing short of three miracles witnessed. Because that is how real miracles happen.

Which we suppose brings us to the big question here. Why did we write our story? Why did we record this all to share with you, our reader?

Every step of the way, it was so clear to us that we were not in this alone. We were able to lean on our faith in God. You could look at our story and say that faith had less to do with the outcome than action. It's true that we were tireless in our efforts. We utilized every resource, every contact, every tool at our disposal. No stone was left unturned. We didn't hesitate to ask for help—anyone and everyone whether we knew them or not—and we gladly accepted every offer. It is what we had to do, and so, we did it.

But where did those resources, those contacts, those tools come from? What gave us the clarity and calm in the chaos to see what needed to be done? The assurance, the patience, the trust? What provided the fortitude to push through the sleepless nights? What delivered Hanna the strength and courage to carry blindly on? What motivated the stranger to extend a helping hand? To us, it was faith.

Faith is having the sense that there is a higher power, a deeper connecting force within every person on Earth. It is a power so great it defies and challenges comprehension, only making itself understood to those who truly open their eyes, minds, and hearts to its existence. And that power is God.

Beyond feeling and acknowledging that God is there, faith is knowing and trusting that God is there *for us*. Like a parent loves a child, God's love for us is deep, relentless, and unconditional. Having faith is the act of accepting and trusting that love just as wholly as it is given. Doing so will change you. It will open your heart and allow God to live in you, and everything you do will be rooted in love. It will flow through you upon others, it will connect with the faith of your neighbors, and it will grow stronger with every bond it makes.

Faith is a lifelong journey. It does not shield you from hardship but gives you what is needed to overcome. At times, it may seem as though God has gone silent, but he is always there.

"And we know that in all things God works for the good of those who love Him, who have been called according to His purpose." (Romans 8:28)

This scripture reminds us that we are not alone. When Hanna was locked away, out of our reach, we leaned into our faith more than ever. We prayed for a miracle, and it was delivered. Not in the form of rewinding time or crumbling the walls that held our daughter captive but as the tools we needed when we needed them most. God gave us strength, gave us hope and patience, and opened doors we would have never even known were there. It was not our faith alone that brought Hanna home. It was faith flowing through all of God's people, encouraging His will through the actions of others.

And this is what we hope to pass along to you. Even in the most difficult of circumstances, even when we're drowning, God works through those who have faith. But we have to know when to grab the ladder, hold on to the life preserver, or accept the outreached hand of the stranger there to save us.

A NOTE FROM THE PARENTS ON WRITING *WHEN WE COULD NOT SEE THE MOON*

The pursuit of writing a book has been an incredible journey. What started as an idea became a "calling" to share the role faith played in our fight for our daughter's freedom. This has been a path of humility, generating an indescribable feeling of faith in the goodness of people from every corner of this world we live in.

Once the commitment was made to share our story, the work began. We had a plethora of material to sift through, organize into chronological order, and then prioritize. There were so many moving parts to our efforts and so many details to decide whether to include. The documentation of pictures, texts, emails, letters, WhatsApp messages—even Facebook was used to communicate— was assembled into a 180-page packet to share with our chosen ghostwriter.

We found the process of finding a publisher and writer to be a walk of faith—it's a good thing we had experience listening to God! I reached out to a friend, and ultimately, she connected us with Ballast Books. That is where we found Savannah. We had phone and video interviews throughout the process. Savannah posed a series of questions, and we each sat down and wrote out or verbally shared details of experiences, beliefs, and impressions. All this was in an effort to provide background and an expression of our headspace and emotions during this trying time.

Our daughter, to keep her sanity during her imprisonment, journaled. At first, she wrote on any piece of paper she could get her hands on. Then, she received one of the most important gifts imaginable during this time—an actual journal. These are items we still haven't read, as they are so personal and sacred. She turned her journal over to the writer and talked with Savannah on several occasions. Our daughter supports this book, as she knows our commitment to our calling. However, she is still working through the trauma and had to stay an arm's length away throughout the process.

Still to this day, we have not read her journal. We read her accounts, as you the reader have, as they were written. That opened our eyes to how our daughter's days and experiences paralleled with ours. We relived so many emotions and feelings during the development of this book. We continue to feel so grateful for the many people who helped throughout this journey. We still shake our heads in wonder about what we all were able to accomplish by working together, guided by the hand of faith.

We are so blessed to have found Savannah. She knows us inside and out. She listened to our fears, pain, tears, false starts, and real triumphs—large and small. She learned that we have strong opinions on certain areas we are passionate about. We would revise her chapter drafts or strongly suggest changes; thus, she would rewrite. In every word, there was a reason, background, sometimes debate and compromise, and emotion. She truly listened and left us in awe of how she crafted our experience into the book you are reading.

This is a book of faith, of unconditional love for our daughter, and of how we can overcome the challenges of life if we all just extend our hands and ask for help.

—The parents

A NOTE FROM THE WRITER

Writing is an incredibly personal endeavor. As a writer, I'm used to taking my innermost thoughts, stories I've woven together in my mind, worlds I've created from scratch, and laying them bare on the page for the scrutiny—and, hopefully, enjoyment—of the reader. It's terrifying, to be frank. And if that's how I feel about creating my own work, imagine how I felt being handed the impossible honor and responsibility of bringing this story to life.

Working with these wonderful people—people I now consider a second family—was actually a bit of a happy accident. I wasn't looking for a ghostwriting project at the time. In fact, I was helping the family explore their options for writers to work with. But from the first time we got on a call and they poured their story out to our publishing team, I instantly felt a deeper connection with their project. I said before that it was a "happy accident," but in truth, I think we're all fairly certain it was no accident at all. Sometimes we just find the people we're meant to work with to bring things together. Incidentally, that's largely what this book is about.

The true authors of this book, my "writing partners"—you all know them as Jon and Tracy—couldn't have been more prepared for the task of getting this story to the page. As they outlined in their previous note, they kept a meticulous record of the events from start to finish, and then there were Hanna's journals. The materials were there from the beginning, and through countless hours of video calls—sometimes diving deep into conversations we had no idea would contribute to the creation of this book—I was entrusted with pulling it all together. With taking their story, internalizing it, and bringing it back out in the form of this book. Talk about adding another layer (or five) to the normally solitary and personal task of writing. I couldn't just write from *my* heart to tell this story—I had to write from *theirs*. And trust me when I say that this family has a lot of heart to go around.

I am so honored to have found my way to this project, to be a part of sharing this remarkable message. We all go through times of utter darkness, times when not even the moon is there to light our way. I know many who read this book will have gone through similar times—perhaps worse—and I know that for many, those times still lie ahead. Our hope in writing this book, in sharing this profoundly intimate account of one family's darkest hours, is that it will help others know where to look to find the light, to reach out and grab the hands that are offered when they are needed most. In many ways, the opportunity of writing this book, of working with this incredible family, felt like an offered hand, and I am so grateful to have taken it.

—Savannah Spidalieri

ACKNOWLEDGMENTS

Within the pages of *When We Could Not See the Moon*, we recount a journey marked by anguish, hope, and ultimately triumph. As we reflect on the harrowing ordeal of our daughter's captivity and the many efforts to secure her freedom, we are compelled to express our deepest gratitude to those who played pivotal roles.

First and foremost, we want to acknowledge our daughter for allowing us to tell her story. This was traumatic any way you look at it. She supported the writing of this book in spite of her need to stay at an arm's length. She understood it was what we were called to do. It takes courage to share your most vulnerable experience, and you demonstrated grit and determination to get through it. We love you to the moon and back.

Thank you, Savannah—you are a godsend. Your attentive listening, genuine care, and inspired storytelling have given voice to our experiences. We extend our heartfelt appreciation to Ballast Books for believing in us and transforming our story into reality. Special thanks to Maryanna and Aloha Publishing for their foundational work and for connecting us with Ballast.

None of this would have happened without the countless individuals who played pivotal roles in freeing our daughter, a turning point that ultimately led to the creation of this book. To each and every one of you, we owe a debt of gratitude.

To our families, your boundless love and support were a lifeline. We want to especially acknowledge our youngest daughter who lived through this nightmare like we did every second of each day on constant standby and assisted where she could. Her boyfriend, who was her rock, dropped everything to accompany her as they traveled to Egypt as support. Their experiences there seem to only happen in the movies, but they were real. Lonnie, your steadfast presence, prayers, and practical help sustained us through our darkest hours. We also appreciate your creative contributions to the cover of this book.

We were in complete awe of our daughter's friends. Your immediate and unwavering support touched us deeply. We are forever grateful for your kindness and generosity and so indebted to you.

To Chris and Leasa, thank you for loving our daughter like we do—you were rocks in the midst of our storm. A special thank you to Max for connecting us with Sammy, whose translation assistance and support proved invaluable.

Ryan, Melinda, and Kari, your tireless efforts in outreach and communication with government offices were indispensable in securing our daughter's release. Lawrence, Brian, Janet, Nicki, and Brian, your contributions to plan B were imperative. These were a game changer toward our daughter's freedom.

Dom, your outreach to Colin and efforts to gain acknowledgment from the embassy that they were aware of our daughter's situation provided crucial reassurance in our darkest hours when we were still searching for a sign. Ryan and Shawnda, your willingness to drop everything and come to our aid speaks volumes of your compassion and friendship.

To Ahmed—though you barely knew us, your caring actions have left an unforgettable mark on our hearts.

To the angel in the jail who nurtured our daughter through her shock with compassion and concern, may God bless you. We are forever grateful for your presence and care.

To the hundreds who offered prayers of strength and comfort, your collective energy sustained us.

Finally, our deepest gratitude to our attorney whose focused persistence and unwavering commitment ensured our daughter's release. Your exhaustive efforts to leave no stone unturned made the difference. One team.

To each and every one of you, our heartfelt thanks. You have shown us the true meaning of unselfish love. You answered a call for help. Each effort was multiplied by the other, building into a tremendous force connected across the world through faith and goodness to secure our daughter's freedom.

And all praise and glory go to God! Hallelujah. Thank you for loving us, carrying our burdens, and guiding and connecting us through this journey. We will forever serve you.